TOP 50

Memory Verse Lessons

with Games and Activities

These pages may be copied.
Permission is granted to the original buyer of this book to photocopy student materials in this book for use with Sunday school or Bible teaching classes.

ROSEKiDZ®

An imprint of Hendrickson Publishers Marketing, LLC.
Peabody, Massachusetts
www.HendricksonRose.com

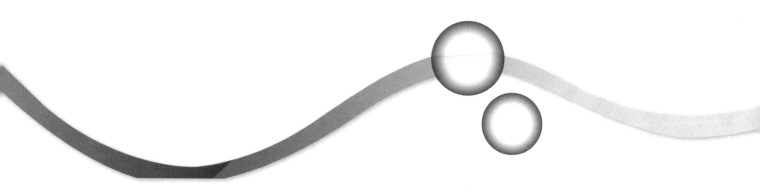

Top 50 Memory Verse Lessons with Games and Activities
©2017, by Hendrickson Publishers Marketing, LLC.

RoseKidz®
An imprint of Hendrickson Publishers Marketing, LLC.
P. O. Box 3473, Peabody
Massachusetts 01961-3473
www.HendricksonRose.com

Register your book at www. HendricksonRose.com/register and receive a free Bible Reference download.

Cover Illustrator: Chad Thompson
Interior Designer: Nancy L. Haskins

ISBN 10: 1-628625-05-8
ISBN 13: 978-1-628625-05-9
RoseKidz® reorder number R50010
RELIGION / Christian Ministry / Children

Table of Contents

Helpful indexing available in back

Introduction

From the Author –

The writing of this book came at an interesting time in my life. Recently diagnosed with cancer, my faith was tested and tried in ways I've never encountered before. Memorizing Scripture has always been important to me – but now it became my lifeline. As I often sat in my room, silently praying, verses such as these came flooding into my mind:

- *Be strong and courageous! Do not tremble or be dismayed, for the LORD your God is with you wherever you go. (Joshua 1:9 NASB)*

- *God is our refuge and strength, a very present help in trouble. (Psalm 46:1 NASB)*

- *Come to me, all you who are weary and burdened, and I will give you rest. (Matthew 11:28)*

As I drove back and forth to treatment and slowly started getting better, verses such as these became my strength and comfort:

- *I can do all things through Him who strengthens me. (Philippians 4:13)*

- *Oh give thanks to the LORD, for He is good, for His loving kindness is everlasting. (Psalm 107:1 NASB)*

Though I was often afraid, I was able to hold onto the hope that is found in Christ because of the verses I had memorized as a child and young adult. The verses that came to my mind during this difficult time proved to be an amazing blessing in my life. Hearing my own children begin to use memory verses in their own life situations was delightful and inspiring. This is what I want for you and the children in your life as well.

The Word of God is alive and active. When we memorize Scripture, we hide God's Word in our heart and it becomes a source of wisdom, inspiration, and strength when we need it the most.

It is our hope that the activities within the pages of this book will make the joy of memorizing Scripture easily accessible and that it will build a life-long habit both for you and for the children you serve and love.

– Lindsey Whitney

How to Use This Book

Each chapter focuses on one key verse and provides several methods and activities for learning the verse. We know that each child learns differently, so we have included activities from a wide range of learning styles such as:

Verbal: Concentrating on the words of the verse, either through writing or talking

Auditory: Using sounds, music, instruments, and songs to help learn Scripture

Kinesthetic: Making sure to get up and move, using games or actions to learn the verse

Visual: Bringing in pictures, images, or art to make verses memorable

Tactile: Creating crafts or projects to coordinate with the verse and help them come alive

Logical: Using puzzles and problem solving to piece a verse together and learn it

Learning Styles

VERBAL AUDITORY KINESTHETIC VISUAL TACTILE LOGICAL

Activities

There are three activities per chapter that come in a wide variety of methods to engage children in different ways.

* **Games** * **Crafts** * **Music** * **Object Lessons** * **Activities** * **Puzzles** * **Food** *

GAME CRAFT MUSIC OBJECT LESSON ACTIVITY PUZZLE FOOD

Each chapter in this book stands alone, so you can go from the beginning to end or jump around to fit your current needs. It's a wonderful resource to use with your existing curriculum, use it as your stand-alone year-long curriculum, or to begin the practice of memorizing Scripture in your classroom or home. Find engaging reproducible activities throughout the book.

VERSATILE

Look for this icon. It tells you that activity can be used with any verse!

The index in the back organizes the materials in a variety of ways, making this book an EASY-TO-USE resource. You will find activities indexed by TYPE, LEARNING STYLE, and THEME.

Easy-to-do reproducible Family Home Devotion letter for each verse. Copy and send this home to help parents keep the learning going.

Chapter 1

Your word is a lamp to my feet,
a light to my path.
    – Psalm 119:105

Theme:
God guides us

Overview:

The Bible helps us know the right way to go in life and helps us to make good decisions. It shines a light on the path we should take in life.

Supplies:

- Black construction paper
- Clear contact paper
- Small pieces of tissue paper

LEARNING STYLES		TYPE
VISUAL	TACTILE	CRAFT

Activity 1

Stain Glass Candle Craft

Step #1: Draw a simple candle outline on a piece of black construction paper. Cut out the candle. Cut out strips from the black construction paper to form a frame around the candle.

Step #2: Cut a piece of contact paper and place the black construction paper candle and frame onto the sticky side of a piece of contact paper.

Step #3: Place small pieces of colored tissue paper in the spaces to create a stained glass effect for the picture. When all the space is covered with tissue paper, place another sheet of contact paper of the complete craft, encasing the black construction paper and contact paper inside. Craft looks especially lovely when hung in a bright window.

Say: Did you know that the Bible tells us that God's Word (the Bible) is a lamp for our feet and a light for our path? Let's read Psalm 119:105 together. This means that the Bible helps us know what to do in life. Today, we're going to make a craft that will remind us that God's Word, the Bible, is a light for our path.

Wrap-up: When we read the Bible, we learn right and wrong, and we learn how to make good decisions. Just like a candle or torch would help us find the path in the dark woods, God's Word helps us choose the right path in life.

Bible Stories for This Activity

- Matthew 4:16: People living in darkness have seen a great light
- Matthew 5:16: Let your light shine
- John 8:12: Jesus is the light of the world
- John 12:36: Become children of the light

Activity 2

Can You Find It in the Dark? Treasure Hunt

Step #1: Prepare the room to be as dark as possible by covering windows with blankets, dark poster board, or black trash bags. Hide candy or another "treasure" somewhere in the room. After explaining the game to the kids, turn out the lights and have them search for the treasure in the dark.

Say: I have hidden a treasure in this room. In just a minute, I will turn out the lights and you will have a chance to search for the treasure.

Step #2: Turn out the lights and have kids search for the treasure in the dark. Allow them to search for about 1 minute without any light source. Then, turn on a candle or flashlight and gather your group around you.

Say: Was it hard searching for the treasure in the dark? *(Allow kids to answer).* Yes! It is hard to know where to look when we don't have any light to guide us. Life can be like that too. It can be hard knowing what to do or what choice to make without anything to guide us. God's Word *(the Bible)* is like a lamp unto our feet or a light unto our path. Just like this flashlight *(or candle)* helps us see which way to go in the dark, the Bible helps us know what to do in life. When we read the Bible, we learn God's commands, we learn right and wrong, and we learn how to make good decisions. Would you like to try the searching game again with a light unto your path?

Step #3: Place the candle/flashlight in a place that brightens the room well and allow children to search for the treasure again. Optionally, you could give each child a small battery operated tea light to carry with them as they search for the treasure. After the treasure is found, gather kids back together as a group.

Say: Was it easier to search with the light or without it? *(Allow kids to answer).* Just like it was easier to search with a light, it's easier to do the right thing in life when we are using a light for our path – God's Word, the Bible. Let's all read the verse together using our flashlight or candle.

Wrap-Up: Shine the light on the prepared poster board and read the verse as a group.

Supplies:

- Battery-operated candle or flashlight
- Blankets, dark poster board, or black trash bags to cover windows
- Candy, gold-coin, or some kind of "treasure" to hide
- Psalm 119:105 written on a large poster board

LEARNING STYLES		TYPE
VISUAL	KINESTHETIC	GAME

Optional: Battery operated tea-lights, one for each child.

Alternative Idea:
Drape several blankets over a table. Have kids complete a puzzle with and without light. Review how difficult it was to do the puzzle with little light.

Bible Stories for Activities 2 and 3

- John 8:12: He who follows Me will not walk in the darkness
- Proverbs 2:4: Search for it like hidden treasure,
- Daniel 6: Daniel chose God's path even when it was hard
- Daniel 3: The three friends chose God's path, even when it was hard

Walking the Right Path

Supplies:

- What Should I Do Cards on page 10
- Large open space for playing
- Construction paper
- Masking tape or painters tape
- Bibles

LEARNING STYLES — KINESTHETIC

TYPE — GAME

Step #1: Prepare a life-size game board for the group. Place pieces of construction paper on the floor with masking or painter's tape, forming a path for the kids to follow. Use at least 30 pieces of construction paper. If you have a large group *(more than 10 kids),* pair them up so they will work and travel the path together. Give each child or group a Bible to use.

Say: Today, we are learning about Psalm 119:105. Would any one like to read that from your Bible? *(Allow kids a chance to read).* This verse means that God's word, the Bible, will show us the right way to go in life. We make a lot of decisions each day. Sometimes it's hard to know the right thing to do. The Bible gives us wisdom, helps us make good decisions, and keeps us on the right path in life. We're going to be playing a game that moves us along a path. I will ask you a question and give you a verse to read from your Bible. Your job is to look up the verse and give us the answer that will keep us on the right path. Before we get started, let's all say the memory verse together.

Step #2: After saying the memory verse as a group, play the game using the cards provided. When one player/team reaches the end of the construction paper path, they are declared the winner.

Wrap-Up: Just like we used God's Word to help us along this path, we can use the Bible in our lives every day to help us make right decisions.

At-Home Activity:

Hello! Today in church, we learned all about Psalm 119:105. This verse tells us that God's Word, the Bible, is a light unto our path. This means, that the Bible helps us know the right way to go in life and helps us to make good decisions. This week, you can continue to help your child(ren) learn the memory verse with the following activity.

Step #1: Trace your child's feet or shoes onto a piece of construction paper.

Step #2: Write the memory verse inside the feet.

Step #3: Hang your work of art near the door to your home and practice it as a family on your way out the door each day.

Your word is a lamp to my feet, a light to my path. - Psalm 119:105

Chapter 1 - Light To My Path

On Sunday morning, you're feeling tired from being up too late. Should you still go to church? Hebrews 10:25	Your mom asked you to clean up your room. Should you obey cheerfully or grumble and complain? Philippians 2:14
You're at a friend's house and they want to watch something you know you're not supposed to be watching. What should you do? Proverbs 11:5-6	You know you're supposed to brush your teeth before you go to bed. Skipping one time won't hurt, right? Proverbs 11:19
You are at school and a friend accidentally rips the page of your brand new book. What should you do? Colossians 3:13	Your brother was mad at you and said some hurtful things. You really want to hurt his feelings to get even. Ephesians 4:29
You've got a big test coming up at the end of this week. Should you start studying now or put it off to the last minute? Proverbs 14:23a	You accidentally broke your aunt's favorite picture frame. Do you tell her the truth or pretend it never happened? Proverbs 28:13
Mom told you to come home from the playground as soon as the sun started to go down. You really want to play for an extra 10 minutes. Ephesians 6:1-3	You just learned about tithing and you plan on starting....soon. But right now, you really want to keep all your money for yourself. 1 Timothy 6:10
You've got a problem in school and you're not sure what to do. Your parents give you some advice. Should you listen? Proverbs 12:15	Kids at school are talking about what it takes to get to heaven. They said as long as you are "mostly good", you can go to heaven. What should you say? John 14:6
Your cousin told you that God doesn't really care about us. He doesn't even listen to us when we pray. Is this true? 1 Peter 5:7	You heard that it's important to read the Bible every day, but you just don't have time for that. Is this okay? Joshua 1:8
One of your friends told you something about another classmate. It was really embarrassing. Should you pass on the rumor? Exodus 23:1	Someone in your church is having a hard time. Your parents want to go over and help with some things, but you think it's a waste of time. Galatians 6:2

Chapter 2

Trust in the LORD with all your heart and lean not on your own understanding.
– Proverbs 3:5 NASB

Theme:
We can trust God

Overview:
We often think we have all the answers, but God knows all things, and he wants what is best for our lives. He can help us make wise choices in life when we trust in him.

Supplies:

- Battery-operated candle or Copies of Heart template on page 14
- 2 pieces of felt
- Ruler (optional)
- Small amount of stuffing
- Scissors
- Fabric glue or hot glue gun
- Puffy paint (optional)

LEARNING STYLES

KINESTHETIC   TACTILE

TYPE

CRAFT

Alternative Idea:
Don't want to go shopping for felt? Use the heart template to cut two hearts from construction paper. Staple the hearts together, leaving a small opening. Stuff with crinkled up paper and finish stapling.

Tip:
You can find low-temp hot glue guns that kids can use themselves.

Activity 1

No Sew Felt Heart Pillow

Step #1: Introduction
Say: The Bible tells us to trust in the Lord. Let's read Proverbs 3:5 together. What do you think that verse means? *(Allow kids to answer).* Thanks for those answers! When we lean on our own understanding, we don't ask God for wisdom or direction. We try to solve our problems all by ourselves. Sometimes that works, but most of the time, it does not. A better idea is to trust in God, who knows all things and wants what is best for our lives. Today, we're going to make a project that will remind us to trust God with all our heart. Before we begin, though, let's say the memory verse as a group.

Step #2: Say the verse as a group. Pass out the copies of the heart template for the kids to use. Instruct them to cut the heart out and trace the heart shape onto a piece of felt. Cut heart shape out of felt. Repeat with second piece of felt.

Step #3: Help the kids glue the hearts together using fabric glue or a hot glue gun. Leave a small opening to put some stuffing inside.

Step #4: Once glue is dry, stuff the heart with poly-fil or another type of stuffing. Finish gluing shut. Optional: Write Proverbs 3:5 on the front of the heart in puffy paint.

Wrap-up: This heart reminds us that God loves us so much and we can trust him with all our hearts. Let's say the memory verse together.

Bible Stories for This Activity

- Psalm 56:3 When I am afraid, I put my trust in you.
- Joshua 6: Joshua trusted God in the battle of Jericho
- John 11: Mary and Martha trusted Jesus to heal their brother

Activity 2

Trust Fall

Step #1: Introduce the trust fall to the kids.

Say: Today, we are learning about a verse from Proverbs. Would anyone like to read Proverbs 3:5 from the Bible for me? *(Allow someone to read)* Sometimes it's hard for us to trust in the Lord, even as adults! However, we can safely say that God always knows what is best for us. In this activity, we will be doing some trusting and leaning. We need to be careful so that our friends stay safe. The activity is called a trust fall.

Step #2: Ask for a volunteer to perform the trust fall. Have them step up and face away from the catchers. Instruct the child who will be falling to close their eyes and fold their arms across their chest, placing hands on their shoulders. Encourage them not to bend their knees when they fall backward.

Step #3: Place the catchers/spotters behind the faller, close enough for them to safely catch the falling child. They should stand shoulder to shoulder, with their arms outstretched in front of them, ready to catch. If you are feeling nervous about the children's ability to catch, lay some pillows on the ground beneath them where the faller might land. On the count of three, have the volunteer lean backwards until they fall into the waiting arms of the catchers.

Step #4: Allow falling child to stand back up and join the group.

Ask: What was it like to fall into the waiting arms of your friends? Was it easy or hard to trust them?

Ask the entire group: How is this activity like trusting God? Does anyone have a story about a time they trusted God?

Say: Sometimes we think we know the best answer, so we lean on our own understanding. We forget to ask God for help making decisions and we make bad decisions.

Step #4: Allow additional volunteers to try the trust fall, being careful to maintain an atmosphere of seriousness so that no one is injured.

Wrap-up: God knows all things, and he wants what is best for our lives. He can help us make wise choices in life when we trust in him.

Supplies:

- Group of kids, at least 6
- Small step stool
- Optional: Pillows

LEARNING STYLES	TYPE
KINESTHETIC	ACTIVITY

Tip:
For more information or to see a trust fall in action, search online for "how to safely do a trust fall".

Bible Stories for Activities 2 and 3

- Genesis 6: Noah trusted God, even when building an ark didn't make sense
- Genesis 21:1-5 Abraham trusted God, even when the wait was long
- Luke 10:27: Love God with all your heart
- 1 Kings 17: Elijah trusted God to provide food, even when it didn't make sense

Supplies:

- Old, broken crayons (paper removed)
- Silicone heart shape mold (craft stores or Amazon)
- Access to oven
- Cookie tray

LEARNING STYLES		TYPE
KINESTHETIC	VISUAL	ACTIVITY

Tip:

Place this tip on a card to send home with families. Or do it ahead of time. Show the children the steps you went through and have them each take home one of the heart crayons as a reminder of the verse.

Melted Crayon Hearts

Step #1: Introduction

Say: Our memory verse for today is Proverbs 3:5. Let's say it all together *(lead kids in saying verse out loud)*. When we trust God with all our heart, we trust him completely. We are willing to obey whatever he says, even if it doesn't make sense to us at first. When we lean on our own understanding, we try to make decisions based on what we know. This isn't always the best choice. God knows all things and can see the big picture, while we can only see a small part. If we want to make wise choices in life, it's best to trust in God and not lean on our own understanding. Let's work on a project today that will remind us to trust God with our whole hearts.

Step #2: Fill the heart shaped mold with crayon pieces. Some people prefer rainbow crayons, while others like filling each cavity with various shades of the same color. Use caution when adding black and brown as these colors can quickly overpower the other colors.

Step #3: Once the crayon mold is filled, place on a cookie tray for added stability and put in a 300 degree oven. Crayons will take approximately 15-25 minutes to melt.

Step #4: Once melted, remove from the oven and let cool completely *(takes a few hours)*. Once cooled, pop from the mold.

Wrap-up: I would have never guessed these hearts would have turned out this way when we first started this project. That's how life is too sometimes – we are often surprised by the plans God has for us. However, we know that God loves us and that's why we can trust him. Let's finish up by saying the memory verse together!

At-Home Activity

Hello! Today in class, we learned all about Proverbs 3:5. This verse tells us to trust God with all our hearts. That's a pretty tough task sometimes. We often want to be in control of our own lives and decisions, but this verse warns us not to lean on our own understanding. This week, you can continue to help your child(ren) learn the memory verse with the following activity.

Step #1: Work together as a family to create a hand motion or body action to coordinate with each word or phrase in the verse.

Step #2: Encourage your children to say the verse with the accompanying actions before they are dismissed from the table at dinner.

Trust in the LORD with all your heart and lean not on your own understanding. - Proverbs 3:5 NASB

** Can be used with any memory verse **

Chapter 2 - All Your Heart

Chapter 3

Therefore, if anyone is in Christ, the new creation has come: The old has gone, the new is here!   - 2 Corinthians 5:17

Theme:
God can transform us

Overview:
When we become a Christian, God begins to transform our lives. He takes the sin from our lives and helps us to become more like Jesus.

Supplies:
• Play dough (enough for each child to have a small lump)
• Creature cards on page 18
• Timer

LEARNING STYLES		TYPE
VISUAL	KINESTHETIC	GAME

Tip:
Don't have any play dough? You can easily make your own salt dough:
  • 1 cup salt
  • 2 cups allpurpose flour
  • 1 cup lukewarm water.
Put all ingredients in a bowl and mix.

Activity 1

New Creation Creatures Race

Step #1: Give each child a small lump of play dough. Read one of the creature cards and set the timer for one minute. Kids will race against the clock to build the creature with their play dough. At the end of 1 minute, take a look at all the new creations. Pick a winner if you like and play again as time permits.

Say: When we become a Christian, God begins to transform our lives. We live to glorify God and to serve him. We begin to kick sin out of our lives and replace it with fruits of the Spirit such as love, joy, peace, and patience. Our transformation isn't always fast, but with God's help, we turn into completely different people. In this game, the transformation is going to happen fast - in only one minute! I will read a creature from these cards and you have one minute to transform your play dough into a whole new creation.

Wrap-up: Our transformation isn't always this fast, but with God's help, we turn into completely different people. Our lives become about serving God and building his kingdom.

Bible Stories for This Activity

• Psalm 119:13 God created us in our mother's womb
• Acts 4:13 Disciples had been transformed by being with Jesus.
• Psalm 51:10 Create in me a new heart

Butterfly Magazine Collage Frame

Step #1: Introduction

Say: When we become a Christian, an amazing thing happens in our lives. God transforms us into a totally new person. He takes the sin from our lives and helps us to become more like Jesus. It's a hard concept to understand, but the caterpillar gives us a pretty good picture of this transformation. When it is ready, a caterpillar builds a chrysalis or cocoon for itself. It stays inside a long time, transforming into something else. When the time is right, it emerges from its chrysalis as a beautiful butterfly. What an amazing transformation! It's still the same creature, but now it can fly and do so much more than it could as a caterpillar. In this craft, we're going to create a frame using butterfly pictures *(and maybe a few caterpillar pictures too)* and then write our memory verse inside that frame. Before we get started, let's say the verse together.

Step #2: Instruct kids to find pictures of butterflies or caterpillars in the provided magazines.

Step #3: Cut out pictures and glue around the edge of a piece of construction paper, forming a type of frame.

Step #4: In the middle of the paper (inside the butterfly frame), instruct the kids to write the words of the memory verse *(2 Corinthians 5:17)*. You may want to write the verse on the board to make it easy for them to copy.

Wrap-up: The transformation of a caterpillar to a butterfly is absolutely amazing! God can do amazing things in our lives too. In the Bible, he helped transform cowards into mighty men of battle and cruel leaders into people of kindness. He can transform us too!

Supplies:

- Garden magazines or catalogs (with pictures of butterflies)
- Nature magazines (with pictures of butterflies)
- Construction paper
- Glue
- Scissors
- Markers

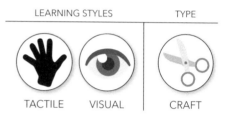

LEARNING STYLES   TYPE

TACTILE   VISUAL   CRAFT

Bonus Activity:
Order caterpillars online and watch as they form chrysalis and emerge as butterflies. The transformation process takes about 3 weeks. Or if you are lucky enough to find them in your area, create a small station for the caterpillar and plenty of sticks with leaves on it. When the butterfly emerges, review this lesson and verse with the class.

Bible Stories for Activities 2 and 3

- Acts 9: Saul's conversion
- Luke 19: Zacchaus changes his ways
- Philippians 3:21: Our bodies will be transformed in heaven
- Romans 12:2 Be transformed by the renewing of your mind

Supplies:

- Books about animal growth, especially insects and frogs
- Alternatively, access to the internet (search online for "animals metamorphosis")

LEARNING STYLES	TYPE
VERBAL	ACTIVITY

Animals that Transform

Step #1: Show the books to the kids. Together, look at the pictures of how animals grow.

Step #2: Discuss how the transformations seen in the books are similar to the transformation we undergo as Christians *(use the questions below to get you started).*

Questions to Ask:

- What kind of changes happened to these creatures?
- In what ways does a person change when they become a Christian?
- Can you still do the things you enjoy after becoming a Christian?
- Can you still have the same friends after becoming a Christian?

Wrap-up: When a person becomes a Christian, their priorities change. The most important thing in their life is God and serving him. Often, we can still do the same things *(hobbies, activities, etc.)* after becoming a Christian, but there are times when we need to cut things out of our lives (inappropriate video games or movies, for example). Let's finish up by praying and asking God to transform our hearts into something that is pleasing to him.

At-Home Activity:

Hello! Today in class we took a closer look at 2 Corinthians 5:17 (you can read it below). This verse is so exciting because it talks about the power of Christ to turn us into something new. Have you become a follower of Jesus yet? What kind of changes did that bring about in your life? If you are a Christian, talk with your children about how God has changed you and continues to change you. If you are not a Christian, maybe now is the time for a fresh start. God has the power to transform you into something new. Just like a caterpillar turns into a butterfly, God can change us into something beautiful and exciting.

**Therefore, if anyone is in Christ, the new creation has come:
The old has gone, the new is here!
- 2 Corinthians 5:17**

Chapter 3 - A New Creation

Bear	Horse	Dragon
Cat	Mouse	Giraffe
Elephant	Squirrel	Dog
Fish	Lizard	Turtle
Rhino	Bird	Butterfly

Chapter 4

I can do all things through him who strengthens me. – Philippians 4:13 NASB

Theme:
God helps us

Overview:
God promises us that we can do all things through Christ. This verse encourages us that God will give us the strength we need in hard times.

Supplies:

- Dry erase board
- Markers and eraser

LEARNING STYLES	TYPE
VERBAL	PUZZLE GAME

Alternative Idea:

Don't want to play a game with the whole class? Use the puzzle found on page 22 instead. In this activity, kids will use a code to figure out the memory verse for the day.

Activity 1

Christ Gave Paul Strength

Step #1: On the board, draw blank lines to represent each of the letters in the following phrase:
Paul trusted God to give him strength when he was hungry and in need.

Step #2: Divide kids into teams and draw the alphabet on the board next to the puzzle.

Say: We're going to play a game to learn more about our memory verse. You will each have a turn to guess a letter. If the letter you guess is in the puzzle, you will earn 100 points for your team.

Step #3: Allow each child to guess a letter, alternating between teams. Fill in the blanks as the letters are guessed. Cross out the letters in the alphabet next to the puzzle as the letters are eliminated. The team who has the most points when the puzzle is solved wins the game.

Wrap-up: Good job on solving the puzzle! Our memory verse comes from the book of Philippians, which was written by a man named Paul. After Paul became a Christian, he did not have an easy life. He was often alone, hungry, cold, or even stuck in prison. However, in this verse, he tells us that he can do all things through Christ who gives him strength. Paul must have felt discouraged and may have wanted to give up telling others about Christ. God gave him the strength to keep on going even when it was hard. Let's all say the memory verse together.

Bible Stories for This Activity

- Philippians 4: 10-19 Paul talks about how God provides
- Isaiah 40:29 God gives strength to the weary

Dancing Raisins

Step #1: Prepare the experiment by pouring water into the glass. Give the raisins to a volunteer child.

Say: God helps us throughout our entire lives. Sometimes he helps us with everyday stuff, like not getting mad at our brother or sister, and sometimes he helps us with bigger stuff, like a sad time in our lives. We're going to do an experiment to see how God helps us through hard things. To begin, can you make these raisins dance in the water?

Step #2: Allow children to drop the raisins in the water. Discuss how they fall flat to the bottom, without "dancing" at all.

Say: Let's imagine that this glass of water is our life without Jesus. Sometimes we try to do things and things just sink or fall flat like these raisins.

Step #3: Pour out the water and fill the glass with soda water or Sprite. Drop the raisins into the glass. Observe how the raisins seem to "dance" by hanging on to the carbonation bubbles.

Say: Now, let's imagine that this glass of soda is our life with Jesus. Suddenly, we are able to do things we didn't think we could do before. Just like Philippians 4:13 tells us, Christ gives us strength to stand strong in hard times.

Wrap-up: It was pretty interesting to see those raisins dance! This verse is a great encouragement to me and I hope it is for you. Let's say the verse a few more times as a group before we head out.

Supplies:

- Raisins,
- Clear Glass,
- Soda Water or Sprite,
- Water

LEARNING STYLES		TYPE
VISUAL	KINESTHETIC	CRAFT

Tip:
To watch this experiment in action, search online for "Dancing Raisins Experiment"

Bible Stories for Activities 2 and 3
- Psalm 22:19 Lord, you are my strength
- Isaiah 12:2 The Lord is my strength
- Ephesians 6:10 Be strong in the Lord
- Psalm 46:1 God is an ever present help during trouble

Supplies:

- Sign language books or access to the internet

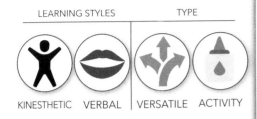

LEARNING STYLES   TYPE

KINESTHETIC   VERBAL | VERSATILE   ACTIVITY

Sign Language

Overview: In this activity, children will use sign language or other motions to make actions for the memory verse.

Step #1: Using a sign language book or a website like aslpro.com, work together to come up with motions for each part of the memory verse. For example:

- I can: Point to self
- Do all things: Make a wide sweeping motion with hands
- Through Christ: Make the sign for Jesus
- Who gives me strength: Make strong arms like a muscle man

Step #2: If you have extra time, take pictures of kids doing signs for each part of the verse and hang them on the walls next week as a review.

Wrap-up: Great job coming up with motions for this verse! I challenge you to show these to your friends and family this week and help them learn this terrific verse as well!

At-Home Activity

Hello! Today, we took a closer look at Philippians 4:13 (you can read it below). This verse is a wonderful source of encouragement and comfort during hard times and a great verse to memorize as a family. This week, you can continue to learn this verse with your child(ren).

Step #1: Write the verse on a piece of construction paper (use big letters).
Step #2: Cut the words apart. Use tape to stick them to a central wall or to the fridge.
Step #3: Each day, say the verse together as a family. Allow your child(ren) to remove one of the words after you have said the verse. Continue practicing until all the words are eliminated and you can see the verse on your own.

I can do all this through Him who strengthens me. - Philippians 4:13 NASB

** Can be used with any memory verse **

Chapter 4 – Philippians 4:13

Use the chart below to decode the following sentence.
Write each corresponding letter above the symbol.

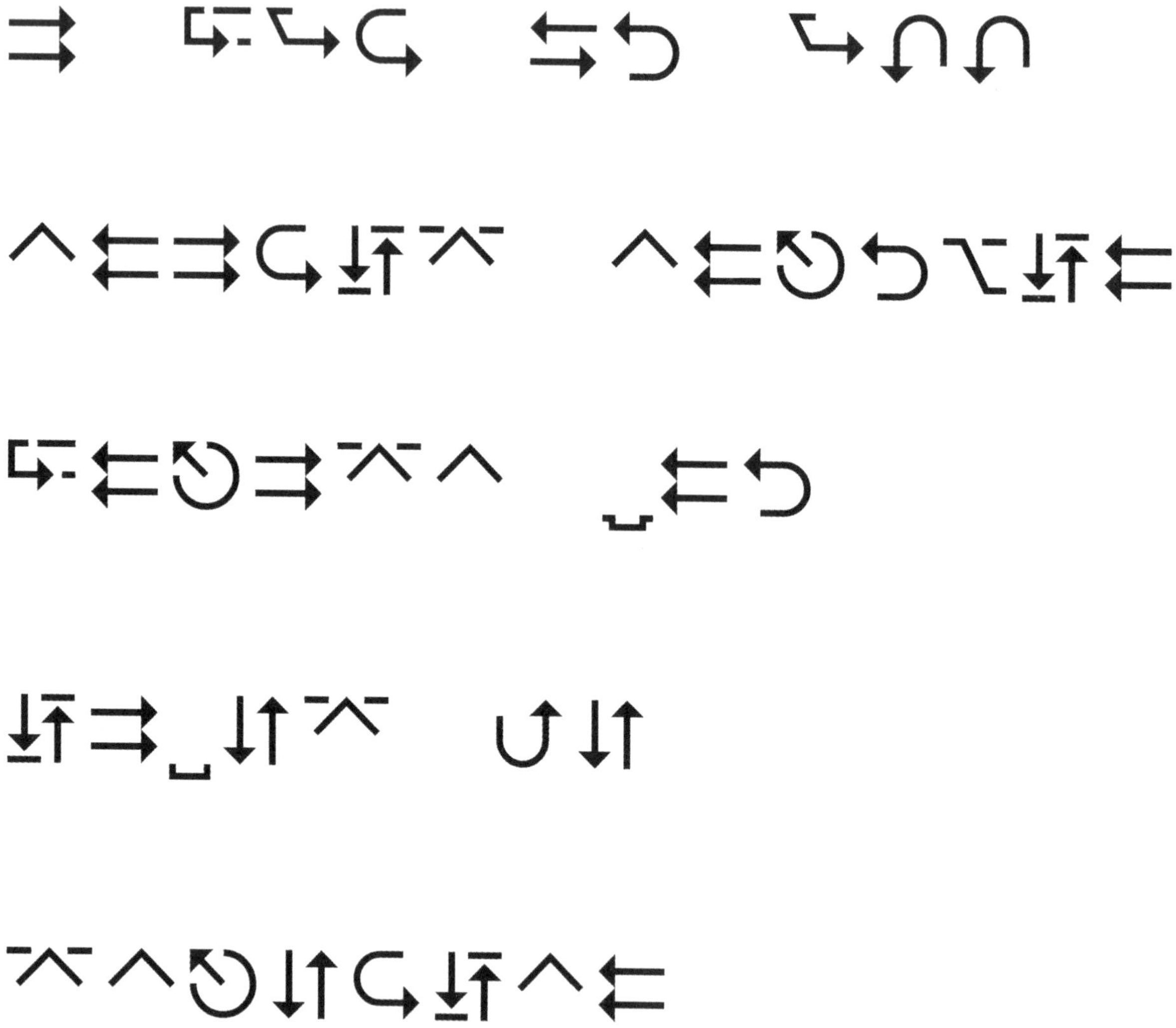

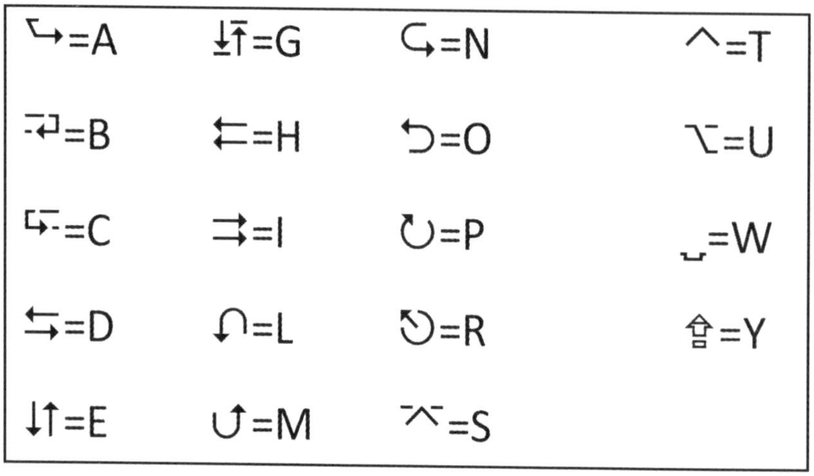

Decoded sentence:

> I CAN DO ALL THINGS THROUGH CHRIST WHICH GIVES ME STRENGTH

Cipher chart:

↳	A	↧↑	G	↰	N	∧	T
(b-symbol)	B	⇇	H	↽	O	↜	U
↳⁻	C	⇉	I	↺	P	‿	W
⇆	D	∩	L	↻	R	⇪	Y
↓↑	E	∪	M	⌢	S		

Supplies:

- Crossword Puzzle on page 26
- Bibles
- Pens or pencils

LEARNING STYLES		TYPE
VERBAL	LOGICAL	PUZZLE

Crossword Puzzle

Step #1: Duplicate the crossword puzzle found on page 26. Make one copy for every two kids.

Step #2: Pair kids up into teams of two and give each team a Bible. Allow them to work together to complete the crossword puzzle.

Wrap-up: It's amazing how much the Bible talks about wisdom. Wisdom has so many benefits and it helps to become the people God wants us to be, loving life and showing peace and mercy to others. I'm so glad that God gives wisdom generously to anyone who asks. Let's say the memory verse together.

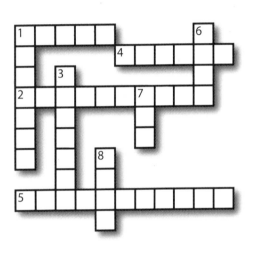

At-Home Activity

Hello! Today in class we learned all about God's wisdom. We took a look at the memory verse James 1:5. Be sure to ask your child what activity he or she liked best. You can continue to learn this verse with your child this week.

Step #1: Grab a stack of sticky note pads. Write one word of the verse (found below) on each sticky note. Put the sticky notes somewhere where the whole family will see it each day (on the fridge, going up the stairs, on the hallway mirror). Encourage family members to read the verse and say it out loud when they see it. Remove one sticky note each day. At the end of the week, see who can still say the complete verse, filling in the blanks where the sticky notes have been removed.

If any of you lacks wisdom, let him ask God, who gives to all generously without finding fault.
- James 1:5

** Could be used with any memory verse **

Chapter 5 - Wisdom

Clues (NIV)

Across

2. God gives wisdom,_____, and happiness (Ecclesiastes 2:26)

7. The mouth of the _____ utter wisdom (Psalm 37:30)

9. Who puts wisdom in your heart (Exodus 36:2)

Down

1. God will give wisdom without _____. (James 1:5)

3. How will God give wisdom? (James 1:5)

4. If anyone _____ wisdom... (James 1:5)

5. Wisdom will _____ you (Proverbs 1:7)

6. Who despises wisdom and knowledge (Proverbs 1:7)

7. The mouths of the _____ utter wisdom (Psalm 37:30)

8. Who should you ask for wisdom? (James 1:5)

9. Who puts wisdom in your heart (Exodus 36:2)

Chapter 6

Jesus answered, "I am the way and the truth and the life. No one comes to the Father except through me.
– John 14:6

Overview:

There is only one way to God and that is through Jesus. Jesus says there is only one way to God and that is through him. He is the way, the truth, and the life.

Supplies:

- Video camera or camera phone

LEARNING STYLES		TYPE
VERBAL	ACTIVITY	VERSATILE

Activity 1

Lights! Camera! Action!

Step #1: Work together with children to make up motions for the memory verse. You can find examples of sign language at www.aslpro.com or you can make up your own. For example:

- I am the way: Put arms out straight to indicate a path or road
- I am the truth: Form a "T" with two hands
- I am the life: Place hands over heart and indicate a heart beating
- No man: Shake head "no"
- Comes to the father: Make a "come on" motion by cupping hands toward body
- Except through me: Point to the sky to indicate Jesus

Step #2: Once you have decided on the motions and practiced them a few times, pull out the camera or phone and record the little movie stars at work!

Step #3: Watch the video together on a regular basis to keep the memory verse fresh in their minds.

Wrap-up: Wow! You guys are serious movie stars. This was a lot of fun making this video together and I hope it helps us remember our memory verse for this week!

Bible Stories for This Activity

- Psalms 18:28 God turns darkness into light.
- Ephesians 5:7-14 Live as children of light.

Activity 2

I am the Way
(Making it through the Maze)

Step #1: Set up a playing area about 10 feet by 10 feet, marking the edges with the yarn or rope. Fill the playing area with objects, leaving room for a child to be able to walk through from one side to the other. Fifteen objects are usually a good amount, but you can increase or decrease the amount based on the age of the child.

Step #2: Set the timer for 1 minute and blindfold the first child who will be attempting to cross through the maze. Have them try to walk through the playing area without any direction or help from others. As soon as they step or bump into an object, bring them back to the starting line to try again.

Step #3: This time, instruct them to listen to your voice as you guide them along the way. Once they have successfully navigated through the playing area maze, discuss the difference between trying to get through the maze with and without help knowing the way.

Wrap-up: It was hard to find your way with no direction, wasn't it? Sometimes, that's how life is too! It's hard to find the right way. Thankfully, Jesus gives us instructions for living in the pages of the Bible and he reminds us in John 14:6 that He is the way. Let's say the verse together!"

Supplies:

- Rope or yarn
- Blindfold (a scarf or bandana works great)
- Random objects from around the house or room (bucket, doll, blocks, etc.)
- Timer

LEARNING STYLES	TYPE	
KINESTHETIC	GAME	ACTIVITY

Bible Stories for Activities 2 and 3

- John 11:25 Jesus is the resurrection and the life
- John 1:4 Jesus is life
- Acts 4:12 We are saved through Christ alone
- Romans 10:9-10 Salvation through believing in Jesus

Supplies:

- Is that the Truth? Game cards on page 30
- Scissors

LEARNING STYLES	TYPE
VERBAL	GAME

Activity 3

Is that the Truth? Card Game

Step #1: Copy the cards from page 30 .

Step #2: Cut out the cards and lay them on the table, face down.

Step #3: Have a child pick one by pointing to it. Read the card aloud and have the child *(or children)* guess whether that card is true or not. *(Answers are found at the bottom of the card.)* Play a few rounds, as long as the children remain interested.

Wrap-up: Sometimes it's hard to know the truth, isn't it? Some of these cards were really tricky! It's nice to know that everything we read in the Bible is true. In fact, Jesus tells us in our memory verse that he is the way and the **truth**. Let's say the Bible verse together!"

At-Home Activity

Hello! Today in class, we took a closer look at a verse from John 14. In this passage, Jesus was returning to heaven to be with his Father. The disciples were worried that they would never see Jesus again, but Jesus promised that he would come back for them. He told them that he was going to heaven to prepare a place for them. The disciples were worried that they would not know the way to heaven, but Jesus told them that he was the way. In fact, that is our verse today (see below). We can have a place in heaven, just like the disciples, by trusting Jesus, repenting of our sins, and choosing to follow God. This week, talk with your children about what they think heaven might be like. If you could help Jesus design your home in heaven, what would you include? If you have time, encourage each family member to draw a picture of their dream home in heaven. After you complete your drawings, practice the memory verse together.

**Jesus answered, "I am the way and the truth and the life.
No one comes to the Father except through me. - John 14:6**

** Would work with any memory verse **

Chapter 6 – Is That The Truth?

A crocodile can stick its tongue out. (False)	Everyone's tongue print is different. (True)	A shark can blink with both eyes. (True)
The whale has the largest eyes in the world. (False)	A shrimp's heart is in its tail. (False)	A butterfly's taste receptors are in their feet. (True)
A hippo can run over 22 miles an hour. (False)	One ingredient in dynamite is peanuts. (True)	Applesauce was the first food eaten in space. (True)
A bat can eat 3,000 mosquitoes a night. (True)	Dolphins can hear sounds from 15 miles away. (True)	New Zealand has more sheep than people. (True)

Chapter 7

For all have sinned and fall short
of the glory of God.
                        - Romans 3:23

Overview:

We all have sinned. Sin blocks us from having a
relationship with God. Jesus provides a way for us to
be close to God and be forgiven of our sins.

Supplies:

- Sidewalk chalk
  (if playing outside)
- Construction paper and
  masking tape
  (if playing inside)
- Marker
- Bible

LEARNING STYLES	TYPE	
KINESTHETIC	GAME	VERSATILE

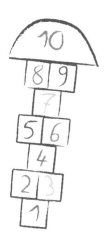

Activity 1

Memory Verse
Hopscotch Game

Step #1: Prepare the hopscotch game by drawing a traditional
hopscotch grid. Draw on pavement with the chalk if playing
outside. Tape pieces of construction paper into a grid if playing
inside (make sure the paper is taped to the floor). There should
be one square for each word of the memory verse.

Step #2: Write one word in each square on the grid.

Say: We are going to play a little game of hopscotch. As
you put your feet on each of these squares, be sure to say
the word that is written there. When you are finished with
the hopscotch, you will have said the memory verse for this
week.

Step #3: Allow each child to complete the game. If you want
to increase the difficulty level, erase words after each round
by pouring water on the chalk (outside) or removing the
construction paper, but leaving a tape outline where the square
was.

Wrap-up: This was a lot of fun and a great way to learn the
memory verse for this week. If you have space, I would
encourage you to recreate this hopscotch game at home and
show your family what fun it is to learn God's Word!

Bible Stories for This Activity

- Romans 3:9 Everyone is under sin
- Ecclesiastes 7:20 There is no good man on earth
- Romans 3:10 There is no one righteous

Activity 2

Jump the River
(Crossing the Sin Chasm)

Step #1: Lay the ropes on the ground, parallel to each other, about 1 foot apart.

Step #2: Gather the kids together and have them line up behind one of the ropes.

Say: The Bible tells us that all have sinned and fallen short of God's glory. Let's imagine that on the other side of these ropes is God's presence. Your job is to jump over both ropes in order to land in God's presence.

Step #3: Allow kids to jump over the two ropes. Have them sit on the side after they have jumped in order to make room for others to jump.

Say: That actually seemed pretty easy. The trouble is, that our sin separates us from God. Our memory verse today says that all have sinned. Can you think of any sin you might have done this week?

Step #4: As the kids answer with various types of sin, move the two ropes further and further apart, until it would be impossible for kids to jump over the sin chasm.

Say: Just like your sins moved these two ropes further apart, our sin moves us further and further away from God. *(Allow kids to answer).* Does anyone want to try to jump the ropes again?

Step #5: Allow kids to attempt to successfully jump again.

Say: Wow. That was a lot harder. Sin causes a big problem in our lives. It separates us from God and keeps us out of heaven. Thankfully, that's not the end of the story. God sent his son, Jesus, to get rid of the sin in our lives. Jesus had to die for our sins, and by doing so, he got rid of the separation sin created.

Step #6: Move the ropes closer together again.

Say: By accepting Jesus' gift of salvation, we can be close to God and enter his glory. Anyone want to try jumping the ropes again?

Supplies:

- Two ropes, about 4 feet each
- Large playing area

LEARNING STYLES	TYPE
KINESTHETIC	GAME

Wrap-up: I'm so glad that Jesus made a way for us to be close to God. It's not fun to think about the fact that all have sinned, but it's true. This sin will hurt our relationship with God, but when we confess our sin and repent, God has promised to forgive us and remove it from our life. What good news!

Bible Stories for Activities 2 and 3

- John 3:16 God loved the world so much that he sent Jesus
- 1 John 1:9 If we repent and confess our sins, God will forgive us
- Romans 6:23 Wages of sin is death

Supplies:

- Romans Road Matching Activity Page on page 34
- Bibles
- Pens, pencils

LEARNING STYLES		TYPE
VERBAL	LOGICAL	ACTIVITY

Romans Road Activity Page

Overview: Kids will complete a matching activity page, featuring the verses found in the Romans Road.

Step #1: Make a copy of the activity page on page 34 for each child.

Say: The Romans Road is a set of verses that helps us understand God's good news to rescue us from our sins. Our memory verse for today is part of the Romans Road.

Step #2: Hand out the activity pages. Give each child a Bible as well as a pen or pencil.

Say: Using your Bible, look up the verses listed on this page and match them up with the words on the right.

Step #3: Allow kids to work for 5-10 minutes on the activity page, helping when needed.

Wrap-up: The Romans Road is a great way to share the good news of salvation with our friends and family. By memorizing Romans 3:23 *(our verse for today),* you are making a great step toward being ready to tell others about God's plan to rescue us from sin.

At-Home Activity

Hello! Today in class, we worked on the memory verse Romans 3:23. This is a great verse to learn. It helps us remember that no one is perfect and that we are all in need of God's grace. In order to really drive home the point of this verse, spend a little time each night this week confessing your sins to each other.

Did you lose their temper and yell? Did you leave someone out on purpose? Share these things with each other, remembering that all have sinned. Pray and ask God for forgiveness and then practice the memory verse together.

All have sinned and fall short of the glory of God.
- Romans 3:23

Chapter 7 - Romans Road

Romans 3:23	For the wages of sin is death, but the gift of God is eternal life in Christ Jesus our Lord.
Romans 3:10	For all have sinned and fall short of the glory of God.
Romans 6:23	If you declare with your mouth, "Jesus is Lord," and believe in your heart that God raised him from the dead, you will be saved.
Romans 5:8	As it is written: There is no one righteous, not even one.
Romans 10:9	Everyone who calls on the name of the Lord will be saved.
Romans 10:13	But God demonstrates his own love for us in this: While we were still sinners, Christ died for us.

Chapter 8

For by grace you have been saved through faith – and this is not from yourselves, it is the gift from God – Ephesians 2:8

Overview:

We are saved from our sins when we trust and believe in God. This is a gift to us given by God. We only have to take it.

Supplies:

- Wrapping paper
- Small or medium sized boxes
- Tape (several dispensers or rolls)
- Scissors
- Two small prizes

LEARNING STYLES

TYPE

KINESTHETIC   ACTIVITY   GAME

Bonus:

Use the coordinating coloring sheet on page 38 to help kids practice and remember the memory verse.

Activity 1

Wrap that Gift Race

Step #1: Give each child a box and a piece of wrapping paper that is big enough to wrap the box.

Say: Today, we are learning about a gift from God. Our memory verse tells us we are saved by faith. This means that we are saved from our sins *(God takes away our sins)* because we trust and believe in God. We can't do anything to win or earn salvation. Rather, it is a gift from God. This is a pretty amazing gift. A lot of other religions tell you that you need to follow special rules or do special rituals in order to earn eternal life, but God offers this freely to anyone who trusts in him. To remind us of this wonderful gift, we're going to play a little wrapping game.

Step #2: Tell the kids that they are to wrap the boxes in front of them. There will be two prizes: one for the fastest wrapping and one for the best wrapped *(prettiest)*. To be eligible for either prize, the box must be completely covered. On the count of three, set the kids loose to wrap those boxes. When the wrapping is complete, pick two winners and distribute the small prizes.

Wrap-up: That was some pretty fast and fancy wrapping! Of course, the gift of salvation doesn't come wrapped up like one of these boxes, but it is still a pretty special gift. I'm so glad that I don't have to earn salvation. If you have not taken the time to trust God for the free gift of salvation, I would love to talk with you more about it today. Let's practice the memory verse together!

Bible Stories for This Activity

- Romans 6:23 Free gift of God is eternal life
- Romans 5:15 The gift of grace comes through Jesus
- 2 Corinthians 9:15: Thanks be to God for His indescribable gift!

Activity 2

Is This a Free Gift?

Step #1: Begin by wrapping the box in one layer of paper. Place a sticky note over the wrapping paper that reads: "If you want this gift, you will have to follow a list of 20 rules."

Step #2: Place another layer of wrapping paper on the box. Place a second sticky note on the wrapping paper that reads: "If you want this gift, you must clean my house every week for 10 years."

Step #3: Place another layer of wrapping paper on the box. Place a third sticky note on the wrapping paper that reads: "If you want this gift, you must pay $10".

Step #4: Place the gift in the corner of the room, where it will not be easily noticed. Once the kids are in the room and settled, pretend to notice the gift.

> **Say:** Wow! This looks really cool. I wonder what's inside it. *(Allow guesses if you'd like)*. I think it's for me since it was here in the room. Wait, there's a note! *(Read the first note out loud to the kids)*. What? What kind of gift is this? I have to PAY for it?? That doesn't seem right. Well, maybe it's a really good gift. Maybe it's worth the $10. Okay, I guess I'll pay, if I can figure out who to pay. Now, let's see what's in it!

Step #5: Unwrap the first layer of the gift and act surprised to find another note. Read the note out loud to the kids.

> **Say:** What? Clean a house? For 10 years? That's just ridiculous. I'm not doing that. I have to pay for a gift and then work for it too? That just doesn't seem right. I'm not going to take this gift, but I wonder what's under this layer of wrapping paper. I'm just going to take a peek.

Step #6: Unwrap the next layer of wrapping paper and read the next note to the kids.

> **Say:** Follow 20 Rules?! I've got enough to do without all this mess. No gift is worth this!

Step #7: Throw the gift in the trash.

Supplies:

- Small box (like a cereal box)
- Wrapping paper
- Marker
- Sticky notes or note cards
- Trash can

LEARNING STYLES	TYPE
VISUAL	OBJECT LESSON

Wrap-up: You know, it certainly wasn't much of a gift if I had to do all that stuff (pay for it, work for it, follow rules) to get it. Sometimes people think God's gift of salvation is like that -we have to do something to earn it. Our verse today tells us that God will take care of all our sins and be our best friend forever and we don't have to do anything in return. That's a great gift! Let's practice our verse together.

Bible Stories for Activities 2 and 3

- James 1:17 Every good gift is from God
- Matthew 7:11 God gives good gifts to his children
- Romans 10:9 If you believe and confess, you will be saved

Supplies:

- Small prize
- Several boxes, in several sizes
- Wrapping paper and wrapping supplies
- Music and music player
- Bible

LEARNING STYLES		TYPE
KINESTHETIC	AUDITORY	GAME

Alternative Idea:

If you do not have access to a music player, you can simply hum as the parcel is passed along.

Tip:

In order to get some extra practice in, you could have the group say the verse together each time the music stops.

Activity 3

Pass the Parcel

Step #1: Prepare the parcel by placing the small prize inside the smallest box. Wrap this box and then place it inside another box. Wrap the next size box and then place the wrapped box inside another box. Continue this way until you have several layers *(at least 5)* of wrapped boxes prepared.

Step #2: Arrange the children in a circle and give the parcel to one child.

> **Say:** We're going to play a little game with this gift. I'm going to play some music and you're going to pass the box around the circle. When the music stops, whoever is holding the box will get to unwrap it.

Step #3: Start the music and play it for about 10-20 seconds. Stop the music and have the child holding the box unwrap it.

> **Say:** Goodness! It looks like we're going to have to play another round so we can unwrap this box.

Step #4: Repeat step #3 for each layer of the parcel until finally a child reaches the prize. Celebrate the winner.

Wrap-up: Wow. That was a lot of work to finally get to the inside of that gift! Our memory verse today is about a gift as well. Let me read it for you *(Read Ephesians 2:8 from a Bible)*. This verse tells us that the gift of salvation is a free gift from God. God gives it to us freely when we trust in him. The Bible tells us that we are saved from our sins through grace. Grace means getting something that we don't deserve. We didn't deserve to be saved from our sins. We actually deserve to be punished. But God wanted to rescue us from our sins, so he gave us the free gift of salvation. That's something worth celebrating! Let's practice the memory verse together.

At-Home Activity

Hello! Today in class, we learned all about Ephesians 2:8 and God's free gift of salvation. This week, you can continue to practice the verse by grabbing a coloring sheet and working on it this week as a family.

When it is finished, hang it somewhere where you will see it often. Practice the verse together after dinner or before bed each night.

> **For by grace you have been saved through faith –
> and this is not from yourselves, it is the gift from God.**
> **– Ephesians 2:8, ESV**

FOR BY
GRACE
YOU HAVE BEEN
SAVED
THROUGH FAITH.
AND THIS IS NOT
YOUR OWN DOING;
IT IS THE
GIFT OF GOD.
EPHESIANS 2:8

Chapter 9

Love the LORD our God with all your heart and with all your soul and with all your might. - Deuteronomy 6:5 NASB

Theme:
God wants us to love him.

Overview:
To love God with our whole heart means he is the most important person to us. We are to love him with everything we are and everything we have.

Supplies:

- Scraps of construction paper, torn into small squares
- White cardstock paper
- Heart template, page14 (Optional) – FROM CH.2
- Glue
- Marker

LEARNING STYLES	TYPE
TACTILE	CRAFT

Note:
The melted crayon heart activity from Chapter 2 would also work for this chapter.

Activity 1

I Love You to Pieces Construction Paper Craft

Step #1: Begin by drawing a heart on a piece of white cardstock paper *(use the heart template if you'd like)*. Each child will need a paper with a heart on it.

Step #2: Encourage children to glue small pieces of construction paper inside the heart.

Step #3: At the top of the page, write the phrase: "I Love You to Pieces!" and at the bottom of the page, write the reference for the memory verse (Deuteronomy 6:5).

Wrap-up: This was a fun craft. When we say "I love you to pieces", it's another way of saying, "I love you a whole lot!" In our memory verse today, we learn that God wants us to love him with our whole heart. When we love God with all our heart, it means that he is the most important person to us. Let's use this craft as a reminder to love God with all our hearts.

Bible Stories for This Activity

- Luke 10:27 Love the Lord with all your heart
- Proverbs 17:17 A friend loves at all times

Gather Up the Hearts Race

Step #1: Punch hearts from different colors of construction paper and scatter the hearts all around the room.

Say: Today's verse talks about loving God. Our verse says that we should love God with all our heart, soul, and strength. Let's say the verse all together. In this game, we're going to gather up hearts to remind us to love God. You've got one minute to gather up as many hearts as possible. The person with the most hearts at the end of the game wins.

Step #2: Set the timer for 1 minute and let the kids search for and gather hearts. At the end of one minute, have everyone return to their seats and count their hearts. Declare a winner. Play again if time permits.

Wrap-up: You guys did a great job looking for love *(hearts)* all throughout the room. Please take one of the hearts home with you to remind you to love God with all your heart, soul, and strength.

Supplies:

- Heart hole puncher (available at craft stores)
- Construction paper, various colors
- Timer, watch, or clock

LEARNING STYLES	TYPE
KINESTHETIC	GAME

Alternative Idea:
If you do not have access to a heart hole puncher, you can cut out hearts from the template on page 42.

Tip:
If you are playing with multiple ages, assign each age group a specific color so the little ones will have a better chance at being able to gather up hearts.

Bible Stories for Activities 2 and 3

- Matthew 6:24-25 No one can serve two masters
- John 14:23 Whoever loves me will keep my commandments
- Proverbs 23:26: Give God your heart
- Jeremiah 29:13 You will find God when you seek him with all your heart

Supplies:

- Small hearts template sheet on page 42
- Cardstock, various colors
- Fine tip markers
- Yarn
- Heart
- Tape
- Hole Punch (Optional)

LEARNING STYLES		TYPE

VISUAL	TACTILE	CRAFT

Heart Memory Verse Garland

Step #1: Make several copies of the heart template sheet on various colors of cardstock. Each child needs at least 11 hearts to make the garland.

Say: Today, we're going to make a decoration to help us remember and practice our memory verse. We're going to shorten the verse just a bit to help it fit better on our garland.

Step #2: Write the following verse on the board and instruct the children to write one word on each heart.
Write: Love God with all your heart, soul, and strength. Deuteronomy 6:5

Step #3: After the words are written on the hearts, have the students cut the hearts out. Tape the hearts onto a long piece of yarn *(in order)* to make a garland. Alternatively, you could hole punch the tops of the hearts and thread the yard through the holes to create a garland.

Wrap-up: You guys did a great job making these garlands. Whether you memorize the long version or the short version of the verse, the message is still the same – we are to love God with everything we are and everything we have. God should be the most important thing in life to us. Let's practice the verse together.

At-Home Activity

Hello! Today in class we took a closer look at the verse Deuteronomy 6:5. It's a pretty important verse. The same words are written in both the Old Testament (Deut 6:5) and in the New Testament (Luke 10:27). You can continue to help your child memorize this key verse this week with a fun game. Gather up a laundry basket, a small ball (or rolled up pair of socks) and follow the instructions below.

Have a family member stand about one foot away from a laundry basket. Have them say the verse out loud and then toss in the ball (or socks). If they make it into the basket successfully, move the basket about a foot further away. Repeat the verse and toss again. If the toss is successful, move the basket further. Play until a shot is missed. Repeat the game with each family member. Whoever can say the verse and make the shot successfully the most times in a row is declared the winner!

Love the LORD your God with all your heart and with all your soul and with all your might.
- Deuteronomy 6:5 NASB

** CAN WORK WITH ANY VERSE **

Chapter 9 - Love the Lord

Chapter 10

Love your neighbor as yourself.
– Matthew 22:39

Theme:
God wants us to love others.

Overview:
God calls us to love our neighbors. We need to reach out to those around us in the love of God.

Supplies:
- Small flower pots
- Paint, paint brushes
- Smocks
- Water for rinsing brushes
- Seeds for easy-grow flowers
- Potting soil

LEARNING STYLES	TYPE
TACTILE	CRAFT

Alternative idea:
Don't want to get into the mess of painting? Let the kids decorate their flower pots with markers, stick on jewels, or stickers instead.

Activity 1

Just Like This Plant.. Love for a Neighbor Grows

Step #1: Distribute a small flower pot to each child. Encourage kids to decorate their pot with things they would see around their neighborhood, such as houses, people, and trees. If they have room, include the reference (Matthew 22:39) for this week's verse.

Step #2: After they are done decorating, help each child fill their pot with soil. Plant 2-3 flower seeds in the soil and water it just a bit.

Say: How long do you think it will take for this flower to grow and bloom? *(Allow kids to answer)* Do you think it will spring up into a beautiful flower tomorrow? No, of course not. It takes time for a plant to grow, just like it takes time for relationships to grow.

Wrap-up: God wants us to love our neighbor, but it's not always easy to know how to do that. We have to get to know our neighbors first! Let this plant serve as a reminder to you to get to know your neighbors slow and steady. Be sure to wave hello when you see them. Ask your parents if you can go for a walk as a family around your neighborhood.

Bible Stories for This Activity

- 1 Peter 4:8 Above all, love each other
- 1 Corinthians 16:14 Do everything in love

Who Is My Neighbor?
Chair Shuffle Game

Step #1: Arrange chairs in a circle and have the kids sit down. The leaders should stand in the middle.

Say: We're going to play a little game today. We're going to pretend that we are all neighbors. I am going to name a feature *(red shoes, brown hair, owns a dog)*, and if that thing is true for you, you have to stand up and swap chairs with someone else.

Step #2: Play one practice round to make sure everyone understands the concept.

Say: Okay, here we go. My neighbors have _____ (fill in some feature).

Step #3: Whoever is left in the middle without a chair calls out the next feature. Remind them to begin the sentence with "My neighbors have _____". After playing several rounds, have everyone sit again in their chairs.

Wrap-up: It was fun to pretend that we were all neighbors. I wonder if any of these things are true about our real neighbors. This week, we are learning the verse Matthew 22:39. Can anyone say that verse for me *(allow volunteers to recite if possible)*. This verse tells us that we should love our neighbor. One way we can love our neighbor is to get to know them and offer to help when they need it. This week, I am going to challenge you to get to know something new about a neighbor. Ask if they have any pets or if they have any hobbies. The more you get to know your neighbors, the more chances you will have to show them love. Let's all practice the verse together!

Supplies:

• Chairs, arranged in a circle (one for each child)

LEARNING STYLES	TYPE
KINESTHETIC	GAME

Bible Stories for Activities 2 and 3

• 1 John 4:7-8 Let us love one another
• John 13:34-35 People will know you are disciples of Christ when you love
• Luke 6:31 Do to others as you would have them do to you
• Luke 10:25-37: Parable of the Good Samaritan

Supplies:

- Note cards, 5 for each team
- Marker
- Large area to run

LEARNING STYLES		TYPE	

KINESTHETIC	VERBAL	VERSATILE	GAME

Note Card Shuffle Relay Race

Step #1: Prepare the note cards for each team by writing one word of the verse on each note card.

Step #2: Divide the kids up into teams. There should be five players on each team.

Say: In this game, we are going to race to gather up words from our verse and put them into order. Before we begin, let's say the memory verse together as a group.

Step #3: After saying the verse a few times as a group, arrange each team in a line. Place the note cards on the opposite side of the room (they should still be in sets of five). Kids will race, one at a time, to the other side of the room, grab a card, and return to their team. The next player will then race and do the same thing (relay race style). When all the cards have been collected, the team will work together to unscramble the words and put them in the correct order. The first team to gather all cards and put them in order, wins.

Wrap-up: That was some quick working! You guys did a great job putting that verse together. Now, it's time to put the verse into action. What are some ways that we can show love to our neighbors this week? (Allow kids to answer). Those are great ideas. Let's pray together and ask God for an opportunity to show love to our neighbors this week.

At-Home Activity

Hello! Today, we learned all about loving our neighbor (see verse below). In our busy, hurry-scurry world, it's tough to show love to our neighbor. Sometimes, we don't even know their names, let alone any troubles they might be having!

This week, why not spend some time in your neighborhood trying to get to know those around you? Take a walk around your block, saying hello to those you encounter. Or, spend some time playing or hanging out in the front yard instead of the backyard. As you hang out in the neighborhood, be sure to practice the memory verse as a family.

Love your neighbor as yourself.
- Matthew 22:39

Be Strong and courageous!

Do not tremble or be dismayed, for the Lord your God is with you wherever you go.

Joshua 1:9

Chapter 11

Do not be anxious about anything, but in every situation, by prayer and petition, with thanksgiving, present your requests to God. – Philippians 4:6)

Theme:
God helps us through prayer

Overview:
We do not need to worry. God has our life in his hands. Trust God and give your worries to him through prayer and he will help you.

Supplies:

- Balloons, already inflated, one per child
- Yarn
- Permanent marker
- Large playing area for running
- Memory verse written on poster board

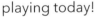

LEARNING STYLES	TYPE
KINESTHETIC	GAME

Wrap-up: That was a pretty loud way to get rid of our worries. When we pray, our worries don't always vanish just like a balloon popping, but the more we learn to trust God, the less we let anxiety fill our lives. Good playing today!

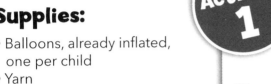
Activity 1

Stomp Out Your (Balloon) Worries Game

Step #1: Hold up the poster for the group to see.
Say: Today, we will be learning a memory verse from the book of Philippians. Let's read it together *(read verse)*. What does it mean to be anxious? *(Allow answer)*. Our verse tells us that we do not need to be anxious *(worried)* about things. Instead, we can give our worries to God through prayer and ask him to help in our situation. Today, we're going to play a little game where we stomp out our worries through prayer.

Step #2: Ask kids to name common worries that they are personally worried about. Write these things down on the inflated balloons *(one worry per balloon)* as the kids say them. When all the balloons are written on, tie one balloon to each child's ankle with the yarn.

Step #3: Lead kids into the large play area.
Say: When we think about something over and over again, sometimes those worries get stuck to us – just like these balloons! However, we can stomp out the worries from our life with prayer. Of course, it doesn't work exactly like this – but it's a fun way to remember our verse! When we start this game, you are going to stomp out the worries tied to the other kids' ankles. When you stomp on a balloon, be sure to say "Praying for you!" Before we get started, let's say the verse together one more time.

Step #4: After practicing the verse one more time, allow the kids to play the game, stomping on each other's balloons and popping them. When all the balloons are popped, gather the kids together again.

Bible Stories for This Activity

- Exodus 14:14 Do not worry, God will fight for you (Crossing the Red Sea)
- Genesis 18:11-14 Abraham and Sarah worried they were too old for children

Push Out the Worry with Prayer

Step #1: Prepare the jars by pouring oil into one *(almost to the top)* and water in the other *(almost to the top)*. Add food coloring to the water if desired. Prepare the labels by writing "worry" on one and "prayer" on the other.

Step #2: Gather the kids together and show them your two jars.

> **Say:** I have a couple of jars here filled with stuff. This first jar (oil) represents the worry in our life. What kind of things do you guys worry about? (Allow kids to answer)

Step #3: As the kids answer, place the "worry" label on the oil jar. Hold up the water jar.

> **Say:** This jar represents prayer. One way that we can show our trust in God is by praying and asking him to help us with situations that we are anxious about or worried about. *(Place the "prayer" label on the jar as you say this)*.

Step #4: Pour some of the oil into the third, empty jar *(about half full)*. Label the jar "My Life".

Say: We can fill our lives up with worry by thinking about things over and over again, but that's not really what God wants for us. He wants us to live in peace. Our memory verse says not to be anxious, but instead to present our requests to God. You might think that adding "prayer" (water) to the "worry" (oil) would just make a big mess, but something interesting happens.

Step #5: Place the "My Life" jar in the pie pan. Slowly begin pouring the water into the jar, allowing time for the oil and water to separate and the oil to float to the top. Continue to pour the water into the jar until all the oil is displaced and spills out over the top.

Wrap-up: The more we pray, trust God, and present our requests to him, the more we push worry out of our lives. It's not always easy and sometimes "worry" tries to sneak back in, but as you can see here – worry and prayer can't exist together. They don't mix. This week, I would encourage you to try to let go of your worries and instead, ask God to help you in your situation. Let's say the memory verse together.

Supplies:

- Oil
- Water
- Three glass jars
- Pie plate or other shallow container
- Blue food coloring (optional)
- Masking tape or labels

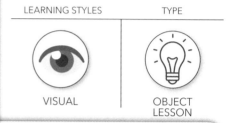

LEARNING STYLES	TYPE
VISUAL	OBJECT LESSON

Bonus Idea:
Send a small jar home with each child with brief instructions on how they can recreate the experiment at home. Use the instructions found on page 50.

Bible Stories for Activities 2 and 3

- Psalm 37:1-7: Do not fret about the wicked
- Proverbs 3:5-6: Trust in the Lord
- Isaiah 12:2 I will trust God and not be afraid
- Philippians 4:13 I can do all things through Christ

Supplies:

- Note cards or small pieces of paper
- Markers or pencils
- Sticky tack or tape
- Wall to display prayer requests on
- Poster with the memory verse written on it

LEARNING STYLES	TYPE
 VERBAL	ACTIVITY

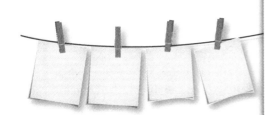

Prayer Wall

Step #1: Hold up the poster with the verse on it and encourage kids to read along with you.

Say: That's a pretty long verse for today! Can anyone tell me what it means? *(Allow kids to answer).* When we are anxious about something, it means we are worried about something. Sometimes we are worried about someone who is sick, a big test that is coming up, a fight we had with a friend, or maybe a show or game we are going to compete in. There are lot of things that we might be anxious about. Thankfully, God said that he will help us through these things. One thing God tells us to do is to present our requests to him through prayer.

Step #2: Hand each child a few note cards and some markers (or pencil). Encourage them to write something that they are worried about on the card. For pre-writers, have them draw a picture. You can caption the picture for them.

Step #3: Work together as a group to hang the note cards up on the designated prayer wall.

Say: This is our new prayer wall. We are going to put our requests here and spend some time praying for them. Next week, we will take a look at them again and see how God has worked in the situation.

Step #4: Bring kids to the prayer wall and have each child touch one of the note cards. Spend time praying for those requests, either by having everyone pray at once or going one by one through the group.

Wrap-up: I love it when we can spend time praying for one another. Let's say the verse one more time together. This week, I would encourage you to try to worry a little less and pray a little more. I will do the same!

At-Home Activity

This week, in class, we learned about worry and being anxious (you can find the verse below). Maybe you can relate? Often, in life, we try to solve all our problems on our own, but God says there is a better way. Instead of being anxious, God invites us to present our requests to him. Sometimes, this is easier said than done! Still, we know that God is infinitely more capable of solving our problems and providing for our needs than we are on our own. This week, perhaps you can spend some time as a family talking about the worries you have. Write down each worry on a note card and then spend time praying about the situation. After you have finished praying as a family, practice saying the memory verse together.

**Do not be anxious about anything, but in every situation,
by prayer and petition, with thanksgiving, present your requests to God.
- Philippians 4:6**

Chapter 11 - No Worries Home Devotion

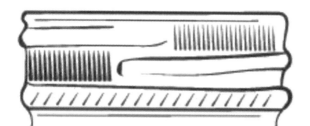

**Push Out Your Worries
Science Experiment**

Fill jar ½ full with oil. The oil represents worry in our lives. Slowly pour water into the jar. The water represents prayer. The more we add prayer to our lives, the less we allow worry to stay around. Continue to pour in water until all the oil floats to the top and spills out of the jar. Worry and prayer don't mix. Fill your life with prayer!

Do not be anxious about anything, but in every situation, by prayer and petition, with thanksgiving, present your requests to God.

Philippians 4:6

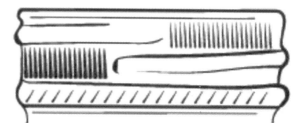

**Push Out Your Worries
Science Experiment**

Fill jar ½ full with oil. The oil represents worry in our lives. Slowly pour water into the jar. The water represents prayer. The more we add prayer to our lives, the less we allow worry to stay around. Continue to pour in water until all the oil floats to the top and spills out of the jar. Worry and prayer don't mix. Fill your life with prayer!

Do not be anxious about anything, but in every situation, by prayer and petition, with thanksgiving, present your requests to God.

Philippians 4:6

Chapter 12

In the beginning, God created the heavens and the earth.
– Genesis 1:1

Overview:
God created everything we see in nature and all of us. Give thanks to God often for all the wonderful things he has made.

Supplies:

- Small, flat things collected from outside such as leaves, twigs, grass, feathers, flowers, etc.
- Card stock
- Glue
- Markers
- Paper bags (optional)

LEARNING STYLES		TYPE

KINESTHETIC AUDITORY		CRAFT

Alternative Idea:

If the weather does not allow for collecting nature materials, kids can cut pictures of leaves, feathers, flowers, or other nature things from old magazines and catalogs. You could also use the template available on page 54.

Activity 1

Nature Collection and Frame

Step #1: Take the kids outside for a walk and encourage them to collect small flat things that they would like to decorate a picture with later. You may want to want to provide each child a small brown bag for collection.

Say: Did you know that God created everything we see in nature? He created the trees, the animals, the flowers, and even the creatures under the ground! He is amazing. Our verse today tells us that in the beginning of time, God created the heavens and the earth (Genesis 1:1). Let's take a walk outside now and collect some things to make a picture with.

Step #2: After kids have collected a number of things, head back inside and give each child a piece of cardstock. Instruct them to write the memory verse in the middle of the cardstock (you may want to write it on the board for them to copy).

Step #3: After the memory verse is written, have them glue their nature items around the outside of the paper to create a frame.

Wrap-Up: These are some beautiful creations, made with God's creation! Be sure to hang up these nature pictures somewhere in your home so you can practice your memory verse each day. Let's practice one or two times as a group!

Bible Stories for This Activity

- Genesis 1 The Creation account
- Psalm 89:11 The heavens and the earth are the Lord's
- Isaiah 42:5 God made the heavens and the earth

Jump the Circles Memory Verse Game

Step #1: Prepare the game by drawing large circles on the pavement *(large enough for a child to easily fit into when they jump to it)*. Write one word from the verse in each circle. Connect the circles with arrows to give the kids a clear direction on where to jump next. Don't forget the Scripture reference.

Step #2: Gather kids up around the game board.

Say: Today, we're going to learn the very first verse in the Bible. In fact, the verse starts with the words "In the beginning…" At the very beginning of time, God made all things. Everything you see in the sky and everything you see on earth. That is pretty amazing. We're going to play a little jumping game to learn the verse today.

Step #3: Demonstrate to the kids how to jump from circle to circle, saying the words out loud as you land on them. Allow kids to practice several times, starting one right after another. After they have had a few minutes to practice, time each child to see how fast they can make it through the game.

Step #4: If the game does not seem challenging enough, start to erase one word *(with the water)* after each round. Continue to play until all the words are erased.

Wrap-up: This was a fun way to learn our verse today. I'm so glad that God created all things and that he continues to help his creation. He makes the plants to grow and he loves to be involved in the lives of his finest creation – humans!

Supplies:

- Sidewalk chalk
- Section of pavement
- Water (optional)
- Timer

LEARNING STYLES		TYPE
KINESTHETIC	VERBAL	GAME

Alternative Idea:
If you cannot head outside, you can also tape circles or rectangles (made from construction paper) to the floor and play that way.

Bible Stories for Activities 2 and 3

- Acts 17:24 God made the world and all the things in it
- Hebrews 1:10 In the beginning, God made the world
- Revelation 4:11 God created all things
- Colossians 1:16 In him, all things were made

Supplies:

- Large sheet of paper or newsprint (big enough to cover your entire table)
- Crayons
- Large tip marker

LEARNING STYLES	TYPE
TACTILE	CRAFT

Alternative Idea:

If you don't have access to paper that large, you can also have each child draw an individual picture and hang them together, art gallery style.

God Made All Things Giant Mural

Step #1: Lay the large sheet of paper on the table. Distribute the crayons to the kids. In the middle of the paper, write in large letters with the marker "God made the heavens and the earth."

Step #2: Encourage the kids to draw pictures of something that God created that they love.

Step #3: When all the pictures are completed, hang the mural up on the wall for display.

Wrap-up: These are some impressive pictures of the things God created. Some of my favorite things about God's creation are _____ (share your own favorites). Let's practice our memory verse together as we look at each other's pictures.

At-Home Activity

Today in class, we learned about God created the heavens and earth. We took a closer look at Genesis 1:1 (find it below) and began to memorize it. You can continue to help your child(ren) memorize this important verse.

If the weather permits, take a walk outside as a family. Comment on the things about nature that you love. Whenever you come to the end of the block or a road sign, stop and say the verse together as a family.

In the beginning, God created the heavens and the earth.
– Genesis 1:1

Chapter 12 – Nature Frame

God created the heavens and the earth

Genesis 1:1

Chapter 13

The heavens declare the glory of God; the skies proclaim the work of his hands.   – Psalm 19:1

Theme:
God made all things.

Overview:
The heavens tell us how wonderful and powerful God is. He deserves all the glory.

Supplies:

- Cotton balls
- Books about clouds
- Glue
- Blue construction paper
- Markers or pens (to label pictures)
- Poster with verse written on it
- Optional: Cloud chart on page 58

LEARNING STYLES	TYPE
TACTILE	CRAFT

Activity 1

Clouds in the Sky

Step #1: Pass out a stack of cotton balls (about 10) for each child along with some glue and a piece of blue construction paper.

Say: Today, we're going to make a project to remind us of some of the things that God has placed in the sky. Did you know that the Bible tells us that the heavens declare the glory of God? This means that when we look in the sky, we can see how powerful and wonderful God is because of the things he made. Before we get started, let's say the verse together.

Step #2: Hold up the poster for everyone to see. Read the verse together a few times. See if anyone can say the verse without looking at the poster.

Step #3: Show kids pictures of various types of clouds. The most distinctive types of clouds are cirrus, cumulus, stratus, and cumulonimbus. You may want to concentrate on just these four. Encourage kids to replicate what they see in the pictures with the cotton balls. Glue the cotton ball clouds onto the blue construction paper, labeling each one. Make sure there is room to include the memory verse or the Scripture reference on the paper was well.

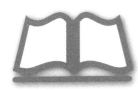

Bible Stories for This Activity

- Genesis 1:1 God created the heavens and the earth
- Genesis 1: Creation account

Stars and Planets Cookie Decorating

Step #1: Prepare the workspace by covering the table with an old sheet or a plastic table cloth. Give each child a smock to wear. Place the frosting within easy reach of the children.

Step #2: Give each child a knife and a few cookies to decorate.

Say: Do you know that when God created everything in the skies, all he had to do was speak and things suddenly began to exist. That is pretty amazing. Our God is very powerful. Our verse today tells us that the skies proclaim the work of God's hands. We can't create quite the same way God can, but we can still have some fun decorating these stars and planets. Let's say our verse a few times and then get to decorating!

Step #3: After saying the verse a few times as a group, allow children to decorate their star and planet cookies. Have the wet wipes ready to clean knives and little hands.

Wrap-up: You guys created a pretty amazing display! You can enjoy one of your cookies and we'll share the rest with family and friends to help them see the glory of God through his creation as well.

Supplies:

- Sugar cookies, pre-made in star shapes and circle shapes
- Frosting, in several colors (put in small bowls or cups)
- Plastic knives
- Wet wipes
- Smocks
- Old sheet or plastic table cloth

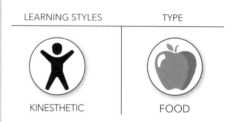

LEARNING STYLES	TYPE
KINESTHETIC	FOOD

Bible Stories for Activities 2 and 3

- Psalm 97:6 The heavens declare his righteousness
- Psalm 8:3-5 Amazed by the sun, moon, and stars
- Romans 1:20 God can be seen in his creation (so men are without excuse)
- Psalm 50:6 The heavens declare God's righteousness.

Stars in the Sky (Stamping or Stickers)

Supplies:

- Star stickers or star stamps
- Silver or gold stamp pad if using stamps
- Black construction paper
- White crayon

LEARNING STYLES	TYPE
TACTILE	CRAFT

Step #1: Distribute a piece of black construction paper to each child. Pass out star stickers or stamps and stamp pad.

Say: Our verse today tells us that the heavens declare God's glory. Have you ever stopped to really look at the stars and the moon? They are amazing! And those are just the things we can easily see. There are also planets, comets, and lots of other really cool things in space. Today, we're going to make a project to remind us of some of the things God has created and placed in the sky.

Step #2: Allow kids to place stars all over their piece of black construction paper. Write the verse across the bottom of the page in white crayon.

Wrap-up: When everyone is finished, have them hold up their works of art and show the class. Practice the verse together as a group several times.

At-Home Activity

Hello! Today, we learned all about the things that are in the sky. Our verse tells us that the heavens declare the glory of God (read the verse below). Indeed, there are some pretty amazing things that happen in the sky. What is your favorite thing to look up and see day or night? Whatever it is, I encourage you to remember that the skies exist to proclaim the work of God's hands -- all of those things were created to point us to God. This week, you can continue to practice the verse with your children.

Step #1: Cut out cloud shapes from a piece of white paper. Write the words of the verse on the clouds.

Step #2: Tape the clouds to the wall in order or hole punch the tops and thread some yarn through to make a fun garland. Practice the verse as a family each day.

The heavens declare the glory of God; the skies proclaim the work of his hands.
- Psalm 19:1

Chapter 13 - Cloud Chart

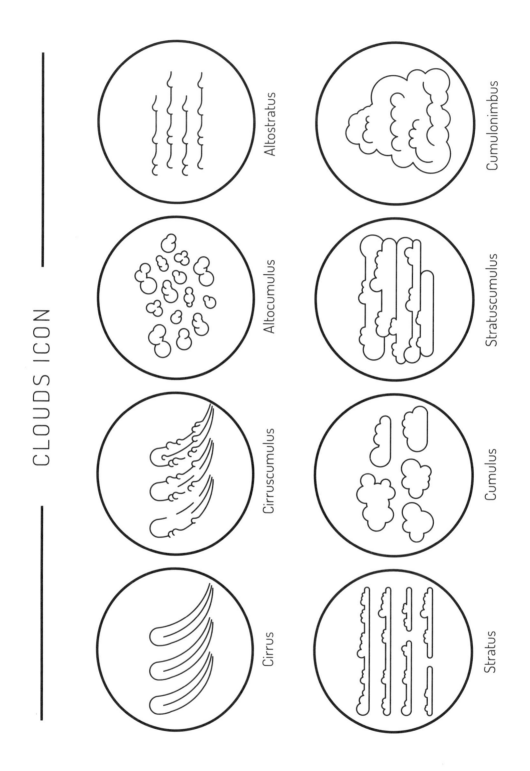

CLOUDS ICON

Altostratus

Cumulonimbus

Altocumulus

Stratuscumulus

Cirruscumulus

Cumulus

Cirrus

Stratus

Chapter 14

Let your light shine before others, that they may see your good deeds and glorify your Father in heaven." – Matthew 5:16

Overview:
When we shine our light before others we are showing that God is the most important thing in our lives.

Supplies:

- Glass jars
- Small tea light candles
- Tissue paper, cut into small squares
- White glue, diluted with water
- Paint brushes
- Wet wipes
- Optional: smocks

LEARNING STYLES	TYPE
TACTILE	CRAFT

Alternative Idea:
If you don't want to gather up glass jars for kids, you can use small clear cups instead. Just be sure to use battery operated tea lights instead of flame ones.

Activity 1

Shine a Light Candle Holder

Step #1: Distribute a jar to each child (or cup) along with a handful of tissue paper squares. Prepare a small bowl of glue for each group by using one-part glue and one part water (to dilute down the glue). Give each child a paint brush (and an optional smock).

Say: Today, we're learning a verse from the book of Matthew. Would anyone like to read it for me? You can find it in Matthew 5:16 *(Allow volunteer to read)*. This verse tells us that we should shine our light in front of others. We can shine our light by being kind to others and doing the right thing, even when it's hard. When we shine our light, it shows others that God is the most important thing in our lives. Let's say the verse together.

Step #2: Help the kids say the verse as a group a few times.

Say: Let's make a craft that will remind us to shine our light. You will paint a little bit of the glue onto your jar (or cup) and then place a piece of tissue paper onto the glue. You can continue to do this until your entire jar is covered. You can even layer tissue paper to create a fun effect.

Step #3: Allow kids to work on their projects, providing wet wipes when needed. When they are finished, give them a small tea light candle to put inside.

Wrap-up: These are some great projects. When you light your candle at home, the light will shine through this tissue paper, reminding us to shine our light for God. Let's say the verse once more as a group!

Bible Stories for This Activity
- 1 John 2:11 If you hate your brother, you walk in darkness
- John 8:12 Jesus is the light of the world

Flashlight Word Hunt

Step #1: Darken the room as much as possible by putting black poster board or black garbage bags over the windows.

Step #2: Tape the words of the memory verse throughout the room *(on the walls, on cupboards, etc).*

Step #3: Have kids line up outside the room. Distribute the flashlights, grouping kids into teams if you do not have enough flashlights for everyone.

Say: Today we're learning about shining our light. When we do good things, we shine our light. This helps others see how God has changed our life. We're going to play a little game, using flashlights to find all the words of the memory verse. When I open up this door, you can head inside to find the words. They are taped up throughout the room. When we find all the words (there are 20 including the reference), we will work together as a group to put the verse in order.

Step #4: Allow the kids to search throughout the room for the words. You might want to keep a checklist to make sure they have found all the words before turning the lights back on. Once all the words are found, turn on the lights and work as a group to put the verse in order. Say the verse together as a group two or three times.

Wrap-up: That was some pretty impressive hunting skills. Aren't you glad that you had a light to help you find those words? Our world can be pretty dark, spiritually. Many of your friends and family might not know about God. They might not have a friendship with him. But you can help them see how great God is by shining your light when you are around them. We shine our light when we do kind things, when we choose to do the right thing (even if it's hard), and when we follow the commands in the Bible. This week, I challenge you to shine your light and be prepared to tell your friends and family about God.

Supplies:

- Several flashlights for the kids to use
- Words of the memory verse, written on note cards
- Tape or sticky tack
- Black poster board or garbage bags (to put over windows)

LEARNING STYLES	TYPE
KINESTHETIC	GAME

Bible Stories for Activities 2 and 3

- 1 Peter 3:15 Be prepared to give an answer for the hope you have
- 2 Peter 2:12 Conduct yourselves with honor so people will glorify God
- John 15:8 It gives God glory when we bear (spiritual) fruit
- Proverbs 4:18 The path of righteousness is like the shining sun

Plug Into the Source

Supplies:

- Light bulb
- Lamp (hidden at first)
- Outlet to plug lamp into
- Optional: Coloring sheet on page 62

LEARNING STYLES | TYPE

VISUAL   LOGICAL | OBJECT LESSON

Step #1: Hold up the light bulb for the kids to see.

Say: Today, our memory verse is all about shining a light for others to see. I thought it would be a good idea to actually bring in a light. The trouble is, I can't get this thing to light up! I tried blowing on it. I tried shaking it. I tried holding it up high, but nothing seems to work! Anyone got any ideas?

Step #2: Allow kids to answer, guiding them toward the fact that the light bulb needs to be plugged into a power source.

Say: I think you're right! This light bulb can't shine on its own. It needs a power source.

Step #3: Bring the lamp out, plug it into the outlet and screw in the light bulb.

Say: Wow! That's a lot better. You know, our lives are kind of the same way. God wants us to shine our light for others, but we can't shine our light unless we are plugged into our power source. What do you think our power source is as Christians? *(Allow kids to answer).* Our power source is God. He gives us the strength to do the right thing, to love others, and to obey him even when it is hard.

Wrap-up: This week, I challenge you to spend some extra time with God, either through reading the Bible or through prayer. Ask him to power you up so that you can shine your light for others. When you do the right thing, people notice and you can tell them about the God you love. Let's say the memory verse together. I've got this coloring sheet we can work on as well - we can use it to help us remember to plug into the source and shine our light for others.

At-Home Activity

Hello! Today in class, we learned about shining our lights in the world. Do you ever get tired of hearing only bad news? This week, make it a point to be a source of light and hope to those you encounter. Here are some ideas to get you started:

- Encourage someone or tell them "good job" after they've done a hard task
- Send a card to someone who you know is sad or sick
- Bake cookies and take them to the neighbors
- Pray as a family for leaders, teachers, or people you know
- Donate toys or clothes to someone in need

Remember to talk about why you are doing these things with your children. We do good so that others will see that God loves them. When we shine our light, people see that God is important to us.

Let your light shine before others, that they may see your good deeds and glorify your Father in heaven. - Matthew 5:16, NIV

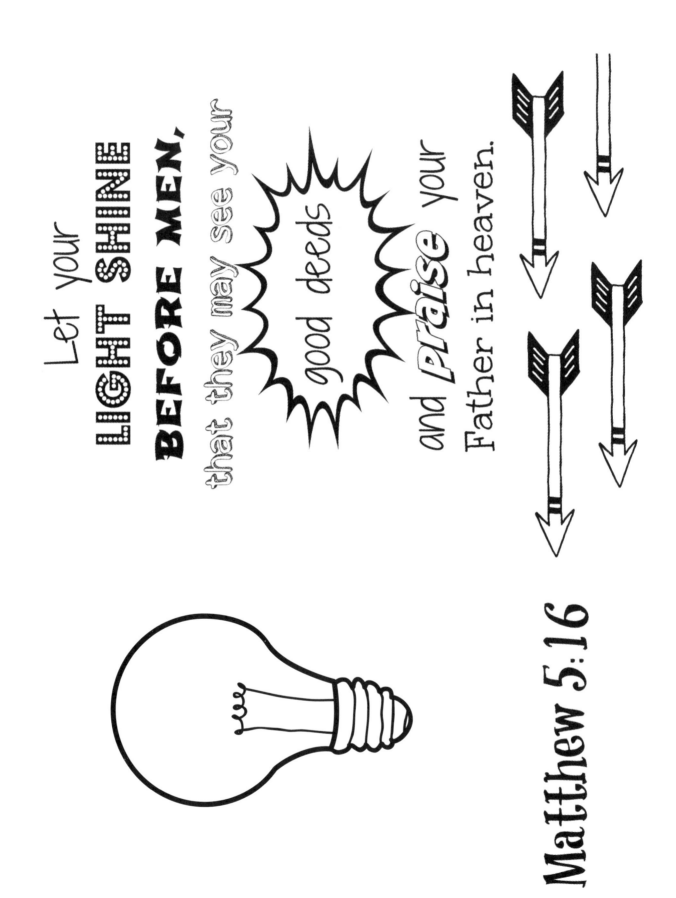

Chapter 15

But seek first his kingdom and his righteousness, and all these things will be given to you as well. – Matthew 6:33

Theme:
God will help us.

Overview:
If we focus on what God wants us to do, he will take care of our needs.

Supplies:

- Oversized clothing that is easy to take on and off
- Small laundry baskets (one for each team)
- Large area for running

LEARNING STYLES	TYPE

KINESTHETIC

GAME

Activity 1

Clothes Basket Relay

Step #1: Set up laundry baskets *(one for each team)* at one end of the playing area. Fill each basket with 5-7 articles of clothing such as oversized T-shirts, hats, scarves, shoes, aprons, and gym shorts.

Say: Today, we're learning a verse from the book of Matthew. This is something that Jesus was teaching to his disciples. To get a better idea about what the verse means, let's take a look at the whole passage.

Step #2: Read Matthew 6:25-34 to the kids.

Say: Jesus told us not to worry about what clothes to wear or what food to eat. God will provide these things for us when we trust him and seek after him first. It's not always easy to put God's kingdom first, but it's the best plan for our lives. We're going to play a little game that will help us remember not to worry about the clothes we will wear.

Step #3: Divide kids up into teams *(4-5 kids per team)*. Demonstrate how to run across the playing area and put on an article of clothing from the basket. Instruct kids to yell, "Seek first his kingdom!" and then return to their team to tag the next player in line. A team wins when everyone has run the race and put on some new clothing.

Wrap-Up: That was a pretty fun game! Sometimes it seems like the clothes we wear are really important, but God says that doing the right thing and telling other people about God is even more important than wearing the latest and greatest clothing. Let's say the first all together a few more times.

Bible Stories for This Activity

- Luke 10:38-42: Mary and Martha host Jesus
- Matthew 6:25-34 Do not worry about your life, but seek God first

Balloon Pop Word Scramble Relay

Step #1: Prepare the activity. Write one word of the verse on each slip of paper. Stick the paper inside a balloon, inflate the balloon, and then tie it up the balloon.

Step #2: Place the balloons on one side of the playing area and divide kids up into teams *(4-5 kids per team)* on the other side of the playing area.

Say: Today we're learning a verse from the book of Matthew. It is something that Jesus said to his disciples and it is important for us too. The verse tells us to seek first the kingdom of God and everything else that we need, will be added to our life. This means that we need to spend time with God and be sure to tell others about him as well. We're going to play a balloon popping game to find the words of the verse and put them in order.

Step #3: Demonstrate to the kids how to play the game by running toward the balloons, grabbing one, and running back to their team. They must then sit on the balloon to pop it, retrieve the word hidden inside and then tag the next person in line. Remind them to keep a hold of the word since they will need it later!

Tip: If the game seems too easy, have the kids try to keep the balloon in the air as they return to their team.

Step #4: Begin the race. Once all the words for the memory verse have been freed from the balloons, gather the kids together to put the words of the verse in order.

Wrap-up: That was some impressive running and popping skills. To finish up, would anyone like to read the verse again? Can anyone say the verse without looking? This week, ask God to show you some opportunities where you can put him first and seek his kingdom.

Supplies:

- Balloons (at least 21)
- Small slips of paper
- Pen or pencil
- Large area to run a relay race in

LEARNING STYLES	TYPE
KINESTHETIC	GAME

Alternative Idea:
If you don't have the space to run a relay race, simply have the kids work as a group to pop the balloons and then put the words in order.

Bible Stories for Activities 2 and 3

- Psalm 34:9-10 Those who seek the Lord lack nothing
- Proverbs 3:9-10 Honor the Lord with your wealth
- Romans 14:17 The kingdom of God is about peace and joy in the Holy Spirit
- Mark 6:30-44: Jesus provides food for a large crowd

Supplies:

- Word Search Puzzle on pages 66
- Pens and pencils

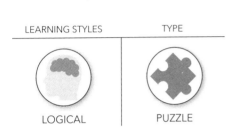

LEARNING STYLES	TYPE
LOGICAL	PUZZLE

Matthew 6 Word Search

Step #1: Make a copy of the word search for each child in your class. Distribute pens and pencils for them to use.

Say: Today, we're learning a verse from the book of Matthew. We can understand the verse a little better when we look at the verses around it. Let's read Matthew 6:25-34 together. We can spend a lot of time worrying about what clothes we're going to wear or what kind of food we're going to eat, but God said that he will provide these things for us when we put him first in our lives. Today, we're going to work on a word search to remind us of the key words in this passage.

Step #2: Allow kids time to work on the word search, helping younger students if they need help. When they are done, say the verse as a group together a few times.

Wrap-up: Nice work on the puzzles, everyone! If anyone would like a spare copy so they can share it with family and friends, be sure to let me know. In the meantime, keep practicing yours first and doing your best to put God first in your life.

At-Home Activity

Hello! Today, we talked about a memory verse found in the book of Matthew (read it below). This is a pretty tough verse to put into practice, because it seems like there is always something to be worrying about! As parents, we try our best to provide for our families and we often make material possessions more important than spending time with God and serving others. This week, I challenge you to put God first in some area of your life. Maybe you can take some time to pray together as a family. Maybe you can spend a few more minutes reading your Bible. Maybe instead of going out to dinner, you can use that money to help a family in need. Whatever you decide, take this opportunity to seek God's kingdom first -- and the things that you need will be added to your life as well.

But seek first his kingdom and his righteousness, and all these things will be given to you as well. - Matthew 6:33

Matthew 6:25-32

```
X Z M V O K G O B U K C E U Z
K J R K J I P R K F K L F I Z
A C Y W R Q F Y A N H O I G K
K N O M O L O S I S R T L A N
Y R H H O H V R S O S H X D D
G P T W D E D Q S L B E O E H
Y O E E R K Q A S U J S E Q P
J R D H N G U V C F Q N R H L
S L V O L L H W Q A R B C U I
B T W L H Q Y Y L I N A K L T
D S N D B I R D S T B W E G M
T N G A Z F R O D H T C W W R
E A T S L N O U Q C B L B W S
Q E V I U P W E P Z Y D O B H
N B A Y L B B T L G I W L D E
```

BIRDS

BODY

CLOTHES

DRINK

EAT

FAITH

FLOWERS

GOD

GRASS

KNOWS

LIFE

NEED

PLANTS

SOLOMON

WEAR

WORRY

Chapter 16

But those who hope in the LORD will renew their strength. They will soar on wings like eagles; they will run and not grow weary, they will walk and not be faint. – Isaiah 40:31

Theme:
God will help us.

Overview:
God promises us to renew our strength when we grow weary. We must place our trust in him.

Supplies:
- Video clip of an eagle soaring
- TV or projector to play clip on

LEARNING STYLES		TYPE
VISUAL	AUDITORY	MUSIC

TIP:
You can find some great on-line clips of eagles in flight by searching "Bald Eagle: Animal videos for children". You might also find some nice footage in nature documentary series.

Activity 1

Soaring like an Eagle Video

Step #1: Set up the video and have it ready for the kids to watch.
Say: Today, we're learning a verse from the book of Isaiah. It mentions an animal that can fly and soar. Does anyone want to take a guess what bird it might be? *(Allow kids to guess).* Our verse today talks about an eagle. It says that those who put their hope in the Lord will soar like an eagle. Let's watch how an eagle soars.
Step #2: Play video for kids.
   Say: Wow. That's some pretty amazing flying, isn't it? God tells us that he will give us strength when we need it. We will be able soar like one of these eagles. Of course, that doesn't mean we will actually be able to fly *(though that would be cool!).* It means that God will help us soar through our problems when we rely on his strength.
Step #3: If possible, share a story about a struggle in your life. Did you try to rely on your own strength? Did you grow weary? Did you depend on God for strength? Be honest with the kids and tell them about the difference trusting God with your problems has made.
Step #4: After your story, ask if any of the kids would like to share their own stories about a time they relied on God for strength. When they are done, say the verse together as a group a few times.

Wrap-Up: I'm still pretty amazed at how those eagles can soar! I know it's not always easy to trust God, but I am so glad that he is there for us when we need strength to get through something. Let's spend some time in prayer and ask God for strength in any difficult situations we might be facing.

Bible Stories for This Activity
- Philippians 4:13 I can do all things through Christ who gives me strength
- Isaiah 40:29 God gives strength to the weary

Balloon in the Air Memory Verse Game

Step #1: Write the entire verse on the dry erase board. Blow up the balloons and tie them. Write the following words on the balloons (one word per balloon): hope, Lord, will, renew strength, soar, wings, eagles, run, not, grow, weary, walk, and faint.

Step #2: Give each child one or two balloons to hold.

Say: Today we're learning a verse from the book of Isaiah. Let's read it together from the board *(read verse together)*. Our balloons don't exactly soar like eagles, but they are going to help us learn the verse!

Step #3: Demonstrate to the kids how to keep a balloon in the air by tapping it upward.

Say: Your goal is to keep your balloon(s) in the air. In a minute, I will say "Go!" and we will all start tapping our balloons to keep them in the air. When the first balloon touches the ground, we will pause the game. That balloon will be taken out of play and the word that is written on the balloon will be erased from the board.

Step #4: Begin the game by yelling "Go!" Carefully watch to see if any balloons touch the ground. Once a balloon touches the ground, pause the game and erase that word. Have the group say the verse all together before beginning the game again. Continue until all the balloons have been taken out of play.

Wrap-up: It wasn't easy to keep those balloons up in the air. I was growing weary just watching you guys try to keep them up! Our verse today tells us that we don't have to grow weary in life because we can put our hope in the Lord. God is big enough to solve all our problems and he wants to help us. Our verse tells us that when we trust in God, we will soar on wings like eagles. Let's pray and ask God to give us strength as we go about our week.

Supplies:

- Balloons (10-20)
- Permanent marker
- Dry erase board with dry erase markers

LEARNING STYLES	TYPE	
KINESTHETIC	GAME	VERSATILE

Bible Stories for Activities 2 and 3

- Psalm 103:5 Your youth is renewed like an eagle
- 1 Kings 18-19 God strengthens Elijah
- Galatians 6:9 Do not grow weary in doing good
- Esther 4: Esther trusts in the Lord for strength and courage

Supplies:

- Eagle craft template on page 70
- Brown, yellow, and blue construction paper
- Brown and yellow markers
- Glue
- Scissors
- Optional: Googly eyes
- Poster with the verse written on it

LEARNING STYLES	TYPE
TACTILE	CRAFT

Tip:
Sample craft pre-made for kids to see

Activity 3

Handprint Eagle Craft

Step #1: Make a copy of the craft template for each child to use.

Say: Today, we're learning a verse from the book of Isaiah. This verse tells us that when we place our hope in the Lord (when we trust God), we will soar like eagles. Let's read the verse together.

Step #2: Hold up the poster and read the verse together as a group.

Say: We're going to make a craft today that will remind us of the verse.

Step #3: Demonstrate how to cut out the template pieces, trace them onto construction paper, and cut out the construction paper pieces. Help kids trace their hands *(for the wings)* onto brown construction paper and cut those out as well.

Step #4: Assemble the pieces together and glue in place on the blue construction paper. Add brown tail feathers to the picture with the brown marker. Draw a yellow beak onto the head of the eagle and add eyes. If there is room, write the verse on the page as well.

Wrap-up: These are some stunning eagles, everyone. Let's practice the verse together a few more times as we hang up our eagle for display.

At-Home Activity

Hello! Today, we talked about a memory verse found in the book of Isaiah (read it below). Do you ever grow weary trying to get everything done? This verse tells us that when we place our hope in the Lord, we will renew our strength. If possible, this week, take a field trip to a place where you can see birds in flight. It might be a local zoo, a place near the water, or maybe through a video online. Observe how easily the birds fly and soar. Do you ever feel like that? Spend some time as a family asking God to help renew your strength and help you to not grow weary as you go about your daily lives.

**But those who hope in the LORD will renew their strength.
They will soar on wings like eagles; they will run and not grow weary,
they will walk and not be faint. – Isaiah 40:31**

Chapter 16 - Eagle Craft

Chapter 17

For God so loved the world that he gave his one and only Son, that whoever believes in him will not perish but have eternal life.

– John 3:16

Overview:

God made a plan to rescue us from our sin because he loves us so much. He sent his son, Jesus, to die on the cross to pay our price for sin.

Supplies:

- White paper plates
- Green and blue paint
- Paint brushes and rinsing water
- Smocks
- Red construction paper
- Glue

LEARNING STYLES	TYPE
TACTILE	CRAFT

Tip:
Don't want to get into the mess of paint? Markers or crayons will work just as well.

Activity 1

God Loves the World Craft

Step #1: Pass out a paper plate to each child. Instruct them to paint *(or color)* a depiction of planet earth onto the plate.

Say: Today, we're learning a verse from the book of John. This is a very important verse to many people. Does anyone have this verse memorized already *(allow kids to answer)*. Let me read it to you.

Step #2: Read John 3:16 from your Bible as kids continue to work on their projects.

Say: This verse tells us all about God's love for us. He loved the world so much that he made a plan to rescue us from our sin. Jesus took the punishment for our sins and because of that, we can be friends with God now, and we can live with him in heaven forever. That's really exciting.

Step #3: When kids are finished painting their earth pictures, have them cut a heart out of red construction paper *(you could use the template from chapter 2)*.

Step #4: Glue the heart in the middle of the globe. Inside the heart, write John 3:16.

Wrap-Up: This craft will remind you of how much God loves every single person in the world. He loves you and he loves me. He doesn't want anyone to perish and spend eternity away from him. If you already believe in Jesus (and are a Christian), that's something to celebrate! If you don't believe in Jesus yet, today is a great day to begin a relationship with him.

Bible Stories for This Activity

- Mark 15: Jesus' crucifixion
- 1 John 4:9: God sent his only son so that we might have eternal life

Activity 2

Sending Love to the World Game

Step #1: Copy the heart template onto several sheets of cardstock. Each team will need different colored hearts. Make 20-30 hearts for each team. Alternatively, you can use a heart hole puncher to cut hearts out of colored cardstock.

Step #2: Gather kids together and show them a few of the hearts.

Say: Today, we're learning all about John 3:16. This is a favorite verse for many people because it tells us how much God loves us and wants a relationship with us. In fact, God loves us so much that he sent his son, Jesus, to take the punishment for our sins. We're going to play a game with hearts today to remind us of God's love. Before we get started, let's say the memory verse together.

Step #3: Scatter the hearts all over the playing area. Set up the globe on one side of the room.

Say: God sent his love to the world through his son Jesus. Today, we're going to pretend to send some love to the world too by collecting all the hearts you see.

Step #4: Divide kids up into teams (3-4 kids per team). Assign a color to each team.

Say: Your job is to collect the hearts that match your team color. You will run out, grab one and only one heart and bring it back here to the world (globe). (If you have a bucket, kids can put the hearts inside the bucket). Then, you can head out to grab another heart. I will set the timer for one minute. At the end of one minute, whoever has the most hearts in this bucket, wins.

Step #5: Allow the kids to play the game for a minute and then count up the hearts, according to color. Declare a winner. Play again if time permits.

Wrap-up: We've got a lot of love around this world! I'm so glad that God loved us so much that he made a plan to rescue us from our sins. Let's say the verse together one more time.

Supplies:

- Heart template on page 42
- Optional: Heart hole puncher (available at craft stores)
- Cardstock in various colors
- Globe

LEARNING STYLES	TYPE
 KINESTHETIC	GAME

Optional:
- Bucket (for collecting hearts)
- Timer
- Large area to run in

Bible Stories for Activities 2 and 3

- 1 John 4:10: This is love – that God sent his son to pay for our sins.
- Psalm 136:26: Give thanks to God for his steadfast love
- John 3:36 Whoever believes in Jesus has eternal life
- Romans 5:8 God demonstrates his love toward us by sending Christ to die

Supplies:

- Car Mirror Hanging Lanyard template on page 74
- Markers or crayons
- Scissors
- Optional: Stickers
- Optional: Laminator
- Dry erase board

LEARNING STYLES   TYPE

TACTILE

CRAFT

VERSATILE

Activity 3

Door Hanger or Car Mirror Lanyard

Step #1: Make several copies of the template on page 74. You may want to copy onto cardstock for a more durable project. Cut pages in half and give each student a single lanyard.

Say: We've got a pretty important verse that we're learning today. This verse tells us God's plan for saving us from our sins. Not only does the verse tell us how God saves us, it also tells us why God saves us. John 3:16 tells us that God loved us so much that he sent his son to die for us. Jesus paid the price for our sins so that we can have a relationship with God forever. That's some seriously good news. Today, we're going to make a craft to hang either on our car mirror or on a door so that we can share this good news with others!

Step #2: Distribute crayons, markers, stickers, or whatever supplies you plan on using for the hangers. Write the memory verse on the board so that everyone can see it. Have kids re-write the verse on their hanging lanyard, decorating as they go.

Step #3: If you have time and the ability, laminate the hangers to make them even more durable.

Wrap-up: This verse has some serious good news packed into it. This is one of the reasons so many people memorize this verse. If you hang this lanyard where others will see it, it will give you a great opportunity to share the good news with others. And it will help you memorize the verse as well!

At-Home Activity

Hello! Today, we learned a memory verse that is very popular – John 3:16 (you can read it below). This is a great verse to memorize as a family because it talks about the heart of Christianity. This verse tells us what it takes to have a relationship with God – believing in Jesus. Have you taken this important step in your faith journey? If so, talk with your children about when you decided to follow Jesus. This week, you can continue to help your child(ren) memorize this powerful verse. Here's how:

Grab a dry erase marker. Write John 3:16 on a mirror that you look at every day. Each day, erase one word. Quiz family members at dinner or on car rides to see if they remember the verse.

Have fun with it! If anyone memorizes the entire verse before it gets erased, they win a prize!

For God so loved the world that he gave his one and only Son, that whoever believes in him shall not perish but have eternal life. – John 3:16

Chapter 17 – Car Mirror Hanging Lanyard

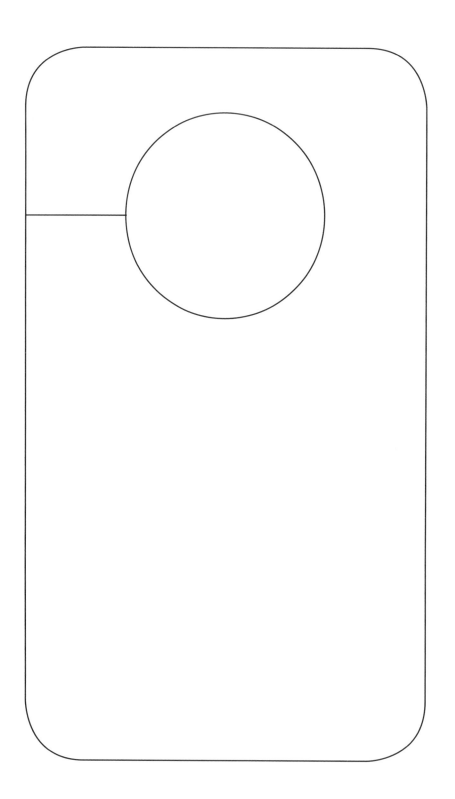

Chapter 18

Be strong and courageous! Do not tremble or be dismayed, for the LORD your God is with you wherever you go.
- Joshua 1:9

Theme:
God will help us.

Overview:
We all feel afraid sometimes. This verse reminds us that God will be with us so we can be strong and courageous even if we feel afraid.

Supplies:

- God Is with Me Medallion template on page 78
- Cardstock
- Yarn
- Markers or crayons
- Hole puncher
- Laminator (optional)

LEARNING STYLES	TYPE
TACTILE	CRAFT

Activity 1

God Is with Me Medallion

Step #1: Make several copies of the template on cardstock. Make sure there is at least one medallion for each child.

Say: Do you ever feel afraid? In our memory verse today, God is talking to Joshua. Joshua has just become the leader to his people and he must have been feeling a little nervous about it! God told him not to be dismayed because God would be with him. Let's read the verse together.

Step #2: Read Joshua 1:9 from the Bible.

Say: We're going to make a craft today that will remind us that God is always with us.

Step #3: Pass out the medallions to the kids and have them color the inside. If you have the time and ability, laminate the medallions. Hole punch the top of each medallion.

Step #4: Cut a piece of yarn big enough to make a necklace for each child. String the yarn through the hole on the medallion and tie in a knot.

Wrap-Up: Now you have a handy reminder of today's memory verse. Let's practice one more time together (say the verse as a group). This week, remember that God is with you wherever you go and he will help you be strong and courageous.

Bible Stories for This Activity

- Philippians 4:13 I can do all things through Christ who gives me strength
- Matthew 28:20 Jesus said, "I am always with you."

Memory Verse Puzzle Scramble

Step #1: Make a copy of the puzzle on page 46 for each child. Cut the puzzle into pieces. If you want the puzzle to be fairly easy for the kids, just cut in between the lines. If you want it to be more challenging, cut in between each word. Put each puzzle in a small plastic bag so it will be ready to go.

Step #2: Give each child a plastic bag full of puzzle pieces.

Say: Today we're learning a verse from the book of Joshua. It is a terrific verse to memorize because it helps us to remember that God is with us when we are scared or afraid. In this verse, God told Joshua to be strong and courageous. Joshua could be brave because God was with him. God is with us too and will help us to be courageous when we are scared.

Step #3: Show kids the copy of the puzzle that is not cut up.

Say: Each of you have a copy of this puzzle in your bag. Mine is still a complete picture, but yours is cut up into pieces. In just a minute, you'll have a chance to put your puzzle together. This first time will be practice and then we'll race against each other after that.

Step #4: Allow kids to assemble the puzzle, helping younger ones if needed. When everyone has their puzzle completed, read the verse together as a group. Ask the kids to scramble up their pieces and then have them race against each other to complete the puzzle.

Wrap-up: That was some great puzzle solving skills. Do you guys ever feel afraid? (Allow kids to answer). Even grown-ups feel afraid sometimes and this verse is a great way to help us remember that God will be with us and we can be strong and courageous because of him. Let's say the verse one more time together.

Supplies:

- Puzzle found on page 46
- Scissors
- Cardstock in various colors (optional)
- Copy of puzzle, not cut into pieces

LEARNING STYLES	TYPE
LOGICAL	GAME

Bonus Idea:
To make the game even more challenging, copy the puzzle on various colors of cardstock. After cutting the paper into pieces, put all the colors together. Assign each child a color. They must find their pieces from the pile and then assemble the puzzle.

Bible Stories for Activities 2 and 3

- Jeremiah 1: 7-8 Do not be afraid, for God is with you
- Psalm 27: 1-2 The Lord is the stronghold of my life
- Joshua 6: Joshua relied on God's strength to win the battle of Jericho
- Esther 4: Esther trusts in the Lord for strength and courage

Supplies:

- Poster of the verse
- A few small prizes (optional)

LEARNING STYLES	TYPE
 KINESTHETIC	ACTIVITY

Activity 3

Feats of Strength Activity

Step #1: Show the kids the poster of today's verse

Say: Our verse today is all about being strong and courageous. In our verse, God was talking to Joshua. God knew that Joshua and the Israelites were about to go into battle and he wanted them to know that he would be with them. Today, we're going to be doing our own feats of strength. I don't think it's exactly what God had in mind, but it will be fun!

Step #2: Divide kids up into pairs

Say: For our first feat of strength, we are going to do some thumb wrestling. Instead of saying "Go", we are going to say the verse together as a group. As soon as we are done saying the verse, you may begin to thumb wrestle!

Step #3: Allow the kids to thumb wrestle for a few minutes, making a big deal about declaring the winner. After a few minutes of thumb wrestling, have the kids line up against a wall.

Say: For our next feat of strength, we are going to see who can hold a squat the longest.

Step #4: Demonstrate how to bend your knees at a 90-degree angle so that you are holding a squat against the wall. Lead the children in saying the verse together and then have kids start squatting. Whoever holds it the longest wins!

Step #5: Pass out small prizes to the winners (optional)

Wrap-up: You guys were very strong and courageous in these feats of strength. Impressive! What kind of things do you think Joshua and the Israelites needed courage for? (Allow answers). I'm so glad that God is always with us.

At-Home Activity

Hello! Today, we learned all about being strong and courageous. As a child, there are plenty of things to be afraid of (the dark, scary noises, mean kids at school, etc.). As an adult, I bet you still find yourself being nervous or dismayed at times. This verse is a wonderful verse to learn as a family because it offers both kids and adults reassurance that God will always be with us. This week, you can continue to learn the verse as a family.

Step #1: Write the verse on a piece of construction paper and put it near the door to your home.
Step #2: Whenever you are putting on shoes or coats to head out, say the verse together as a family.

Be strong and courageous! Do not tremble or be dismayed,
for the Lord your God is with you wherever you go. - Joshua 1:9

Chapter 18 - God is With Me Medallion

Chapter 19

God is our refuge and strength,
a very present help in trouble.
– Psalm 46:1 NASB

Theme:
God will help us.

Overview:
God will be with us whenever we are in trouble.
He will protect us and keeps us safe.

Supplies:

- Chairs, arranged in a circle, one for each child
- Poster prepared with blanks for each word of the memory verse
- Note cards
- Tape
- Music player

LEARNING STYLES   TYPE

KINESTHETIC

GAME   VERSATILE

Activity 1

Musical Memory Verse Chairs

Step #1: Prepare a poster ahead of time, making a blank for each word of the verse. Prepare the note cards by writing one word of the verse on each card.

Step #2: Arrange the chairs in a circle and tape the note cards to the bottom of the chairs. If there are more words than chairs, tape two words to the bottom of some chairs.

Step #3: Have kids sit in chairs. Show them the poster full of blanks.

Say: We're going to work together to complete this poster of the memory verse. Our verse today comes from the book of Psalms. Let me read it for you (Read Psalm 46:1). I'm going to play some music and you will walk around the circle of chairs. When the music stops, sit in the chair nearest to you.

Step #4: Play the music and allow the kids to walk around in a circle for 5-10 seconds. Stop the music and have the kids sit in the chairs. Call on one child to look under their chair. Take the word from under the chair and add it to the poster in the appropriate spot.

Say: Nice job! Now you know how we're going to complete this poster. Let me read the verse to you again and then we'll play another round.

Step #5: Repeat step 4 (you may want to keep a diagram to keep track of which chairs are empty and which still have words taped to them). As the poster gets more filled in, see if kids can place the words in the proper place on their own. Read the verse out loud in between rounds.

Wrap-up: That was certainly an interesting way to make a poster of our memory verse for today. Let's practice the verse out loud together.

Bible Stories for This Activity

- Jeremiah 1: 7-8 Do not be afraid, for God is with you
- Matthew 26:36-44: Jesus prays in the garden before he dies

Activity 2

God Is My Refuge Box Stacking Game

Step #1: Prepare the boxes ahead of time by writing one word of the verse on the side of each box. When the kids arrive, show them the poster of the memory verse.

Say: Our verse today is very comforting. It tells us that God will be with us whenever we are in trouble. He will be our refuge and our strength. Does anyone know what a refuge is? *(Allow kids to answer).* A refuge is a safe place to hide or a place where you will be protected from danger. Back in Bible times, they used to have cities of refuge where you could run and be protected from people who were trying to harm you. We're going to build a little city of refuge as well with these boxes.

Step #2: Show kids the boxes that you have prepared.

Say: Of course, we're not going to stack the boxes up just any which way. We've got to put them in order. I have written the words of the memory verse on these boxes. Your job is to arrange the boxes so that they show the completed memory verse. You can either put them in one long line or you can stack them up pyramid style with the beginning of the verse on top and the end of the verse on the bottom.

Step #3: If needed, demonstrate to the kids how to stack a few boxes. Remind them that they can look at the poster for help. Say the verse together as a group and then allow the kids to stack the boxes.

Say: That was pretty good. I like your city of refuge! Now, let's try to race against the clock and stack the boxes up again. This time, we will try to go as fast as we can!

Step #4: Scramble the boxes up. Say the verse as a group and then start the timer. Have kids stack the boxes as fast as they can. Play again if time permits to make a new high score.

Wrap-Up: You guys did a great job stacking these boxes. I can't believe how fast you could put our memory verse together. Let's say the verse one more time together and then spend some time praying that God will help us if we are having any trouble this week.

Supplies:

- Several boxes (14 if possible)
- Large tip marker
- Poster of the memory verse
- Timer/Stopwatch

LEARNING STYLES	TYPE	
KINESTHETIC	GAME	VERSATILE

Bible Stories for Activities 2 and 3

- Psalm 145:18: The Lord is near to all who call on him
- Psalm 9:9: The Lord is a stronghold
- Job: Job trusted in God even during very difficult times
- Lamentations 3:22-23: God's love never ends

Supplies:

- Poster of the verse
- Copies of card template found on page 82 (optional)
- Stickers
- Construction paper
- Crayons

LEARNING STYLES	TYPE

TACTILE	CRAFT

Activity 3

Encouragement Cards

Step #1: Show the kids the poster of today's verse.

Say: There are many different kinds of verses in the Bible. Some verses tell us what to do. Some help us make good decisions. Some verses, like this one, provide encouragement for us during hard times. Let's read the verse together.

Step #2: Read Psalm 46:1 together from the poster.

Say: This verse tells us that God will shelter us and protect us when we are facing trouble. He will be near us and help us when we need it. Today, we're going to make cards for people who may be facing hard times. I want you to think about a person who might be sad, discouraged, or sick. Let's make them a card using this verse.

Step #3: Pass out the card template for the kids who would like to use it. Some kids might like to write the verse themselves on a construction paper card instead. Provide crayons, markers, and stickers to decorate the cards with.

Step #4: When the kids are finished with their cards, spend some time praying for the people who will receive the cards, asking God to be a very present help to them during their time of trouble.

Wrap-up: Terrific job on the cards. I'm sure these will provide some encouragement to the people you made these for and remind them that God will be with them during their time of trouble.

At-Home Activity

Today in class, we began learning Psalm 46:1 (you can read it below). This verse provides comfort for us during hard times. You can continue learning this verse with your child by using the following actions for each word.

God (point up)
Is our refuge (tent fingers together to symbolize a place of shelter)
And strength (make strong arms)
A very present help (place left palm flat, facing up and right hand on top with thumb's up sign)
In trouble (put hands on face in scared expression)

Practice these motions together as you say the verse out loud. A great time to practice would be just before eating dinner each night.

God is our refuge and strength, a very present help in trouble. – Psalm 46:1 NASB

God is our refuge and strength, a very present help in trouble.

Psaml 46:1

Chapter 20

Give thanks to the LORD, for he is good; his love endures.
 – Psalm 107:1

Overview:
God wants us to remember that he loves us forever! We should be grateful for his love and give thanks to him all the time.

Supplies:

- Music or video player
- Songs about giving thanks to God
- Construction paper
- Crayons

LEARNING STYLES	TYPE
AUDITORY	MUSIC

Tip:
Find songs about giving thanks by searching online for "songs about giving thanks to God."

Some songs to consider:
- Forever by Chris Tomlin
- Don't Be a Turkey by Yancy
- I Just Want to Thank You Lord by Sunday School Jamz
- Better Than Life by Seeds Family Worship

Activity 1

Singing Praise to God

Step #1: Find some simple songs about giving thanks and practice them a few times on your own.

Say: God has given us so much to be thankful for in our lives. What are some things you can give thanks to God for? (Allow kids to answer)

Step #2: Briefly teach the kids a few of the lyrics and motions to the songs you have chosen.

Say: One way we can give thanks to God is through singing. Let's praise the Lord with a few songs.

Step #3: Pass out construction paper and crayons to each of the kids and encourage them to draw pictures of things they are thankful for as you play the music in the background.

Wrap-up: There are so many things we can give thanks for. Let's continue to listen to these songs as we color pictures of the good things God has put in our lives. Feel free to sing along as you color!

Bible Stories for This Activity

- Psalm 106:1 Give thanks to the Lord
- Nehemiah 9:17 God showed loving kindness to the Israelites
- Psalm 63:1-4 Give thanks for God's power and glory

Thankful Tree

Step #1: Cut 1 piece of brown construction paper in half to form a tree trunk. Tape to wall.

Step #2: Cut 1 piece of brown construction into quarters (length-wise) to form branches. Tape to wall, connected to the tree trunk.

Step #3: Make copies of the leaf template and give each child a template to use.

Alternative idea: Use the hole puncher to cut out several leaves from construction paper.

Step #4: Demonstrate to kids how to use the template to trace leaves on construction paper. Pass out scissors and have kids cut out their leaves.

Say: Our verse today is all about giving thanks to the Lord. Let me read it to you. Read Psalm 107:1 from the Bible. Can you guys say it with me? *(Practice saying the verse together a few times).* We're going to make a thankful tree using these leaves.

Step #5: Help kids write things that they are thankful for and then tape the leaves to the tree you created with brown construction paper. Every 5 leaves or so, pause to say the verse together.

Wrap-up: This tree is filled with things that we can give thanks for. Let's pray together now and thank the Lord for his kindness and for all he has given us.

Supplies:

- Leaf template
- Construction paper in various colors
- Brown construction paper
- Tape
- Scissors
- Leaf hole puncher (optional)

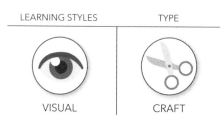

LEARNING STYLES	TYPE
VISUAL	CRAFT

Bible Stories for Activities 2 and 3

- 1 Thessalonians 5:18 Give thanks in all circumstances
- James 1:17 Every good gift is from God
- Psalm 105:1 Give thanks to the Lord
- 1 Timothy 4:4 Everything God created is good

Supplies:

- Watercolor paints
- Ear swabs
- Thank You sheet on page 86
- Poster of the memory verse

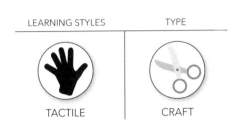

LEARNING STYLES	TYPE
TACTILE	CRAFT

Thank You Pointillism Craft

Step #1: Make copies of the Thank You sheet on page 86 for each child.

Step #2: Set up each child's work space with a set of watercolors, water, the Thank You sheet, and several ear swabs

Say: Our verse today is all about giving thanks to the Lord. Let's say the verse together (read from the poster). We're going to make a craft to help remind us to give thanks to God each day for his loving kindness and for all the good he brings into our lives.

Step #3: Dip an ear swab in water and then in a water color. Demonstrate to the kids how to dab little dots inside the word outline to make a pointillism work of art.

Wrap-up: When everyone is finished, have them hold up their works of art and show the class. Practice the verse together as a group several times.

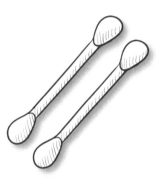

At-Home Activity

Hello! Today in class, we learned about giving thanks to the Lord. You can continue to learn and practice the memory verse with your child(ren) this week (find it below). Here is a fun game you can play as a family to practice giving thanks to the Lord.

Step #1: Have one person start by saying, "I give thanks to God for _____". Have them fill in the blank with a word that starts with the letter "A".

Step #2: Have another person continue the game by saying, "I give thanks to God for _____." Have them fill in the blank with something that starts with the letter "B".

Step #3: Continue in this way, switching from person to person, until you reach the end of the alphabet. For an extra challenge, see if you can remember all the things named before yours.

Give thanks to the LORD, for he is good; his love endures.
- Psalm 107:1

Give thanks to the lord, for he is good; his love endures. - Psalm 107:1

Chapter 21

He who walks with wise men will be wise, but the companion of fools will suffer harm.
– Proverbs 13:20 NASB

Theme: We need to make wise choices about our friends.

Overview:
Who you hang around with makes a big difference in your life. Choice to be with wise people and you will make better choices.

Supplies:
- Copies of Wise Man and Fool cards on page 90
- Scissors (or paper cutter)

LEARNING STYLES	TYPE

KINESTHETIC	GAME

Wrap-up: Just like in our game, a foolish person will subtract from our life, but a wise person adds to it. We should show kindness to everyone, but when we are picking our very best friends, we should look for people who show wisdom. Let's say the verse one more time together.

Activity 1

Wise and Foolish Men

Step #1: Make copies of the Wise Man and Fool cards on page 90. Make at least one set for each child in your class.

Step #2: Cut cards apart. Store in small plastic bags until class time.

Step #3: Pair kids up and give each child a bag of cards.

Say: Today we are talking about a verse from Proverbs. King Solomon wrote most of the book of Proverbs and it is filled with short sayings that give good advice or some kind of truth. Our verse today is Proverbs 13:20. Let me read it for you.

Step #4: Read Proverbs 13:20.

Say: What do you think the difference between a wise man and a fool is? *(Allow kids to answer).* A wise man obeys God, but a fool does whatever he feels like doing. Do you have friends that show wisdom? How about friends that act foolish? The more we hang out with someone, the more we begin to act like them, which is why the Bible tells us to be with people who are making wise decisions. Let's say the verse all together.

Step #5: Instruct the kids to lay their cards out on the table (each pair of kids will mix their cards together), face down. They will take turns picking cards. Each child should keep their own pile of cards. When all the cards are picked, they can add up their points. Each wise man is 10 points, but each foolish man is negative 20 points. Whoever has the most points at the end of the game, wins.

Bible Stories for This Activity

- Matthew 7:24-27: Wise and Foolish Builders
- 1 Kings 3:1-15: Solomon asks for Wisdom

Walking with the Wise

Step #1: Set up cones to make playing area (optional).

Step #2: Place objects in the playing area to serve as obstacles.

Step #3: Arrange several kids inside the playing area. These kids will act as the fools in the game.

Say: Our verse today is all about the difference wise and foolish people make in our lives. When we choose to be friends with wise people (our verse calls it walking with the wise), we will be wise as well. However, if we choose to be friends with foolish people, we will end up suffering harm. What kind of harm might you suffer from being the friend (or companion) of a fool? *(Allow kids to answer).* In this game, we have some "fools" in the playing area. They are going to try to trick the walker into coming near them or near an obstacle.

Step #4: Pick one child to be the first "walker". Place a blindfold on their eyes and stand them at one end of the playing field. Place another child at the other end of the playing field. This child will serve as a "wise friend" helping to guide them through the playing field. They should shout instructions to help navigate them through the playing field.

Step #5: Allow the walker to try to walk through the playing field without running into any of the obstacles or "fools". The "fools" are allowed to yell or try to trick the walker into running into obstacles. They can also reach out and try to grab the "walker." If the "walker" runs into any object or person, their turn is up. Play again as time permits.

Wrap-up: Wow, that was a pretty tough task! When you listened to the fools, you ended up suffering harm, but if you listened only to your wise friend, you made it through the playing field. Sometimes it's hard to sort out all the different things we are hearing, which is why it is important to surround ourselves with friends who are going to help us become wise.

Supplies:

- Blindfold
- Large playing area
- Cones to mark playing area (optional)
- Random objects to serve as obstacles in the playing area

LEARNING STYLES	TYPE
KINESTHETIC	GAME

Bible Stories for Activities 2 and 3

- Psalm 1:1 Do not walk in the council of the wicked
- Proverbs 12:15 The way of fools seems right to them.
- Judges 16 Samson suffered harm when he chose to be friends with Delilah
- Proverbs 12:26 The righteous choose their friends carefully

Craft Stick Memory Verse Puzzle

Supplies:

- Wide craft sticks, at least 20 per child
- Markers
- City panorama silhouettes
- Recycled paper craft stick on white background
- Yarn or ribbon
- Poster of memory verse (or write verse on board)

LEARNING STYLES	TYPE	
LOGICAL	PUZZLE	VERSATILE

Step #1: Distribute 20 craft sticks to each child.

Step #2: Instruct them to write one word of the verse on each stick. If they want, they can arrange them in order and draw a design along the edges to make the puzzle easier to assemble later.

Say: Today, we're learning a verse from the book of Proverbs. Would anyone like to read the verse from the poster (or board) for me? This verse means that we will be affected by the people we choose to hang out with the most. If we walk with the wise, we will become wise too. However, if we choose to be good friends with fools, we will end up suffering harm. Did you ever have a friend who tried to get you to do things that were wrong? *(Allow kids to answer)*. We need to be careful about who we choose to be very good friends with. Our puzzle today will help us to learn the verse and help us to remember to look for wise people to be friends with.

Step #3: Demonstrate how to mix up the craft sticks and then assemble them again as a puzzle. After the kids have had a chance to do their puzzle a few times, hold a race to see who can complete the puzzle the fastest.

Step #4: When you are done with the puzzles, wrap each set of craft sticks with yarn or ribbon for easy carrying.

Wrap-up: You guys did a really good job putting those puzzles together. Aren't you glad that the Bible isn't puzzling? Instead, it is filled with very clear instructions, including our verse today.

At-Home Activity

Hello! Today in class we talked about the difference between surrounding yourself with wise people and surrounding yourself with foolish people. You can find the memory verse below. This is a great opportunity for you to talk with your child(ren) about the difference good and bad influences have made in your life. Was there someone who helped you make wise choices in your life? Was there someone who always seemed to be leading you into trouble? Share a few age-appropriate stories with your kids and encourage them to make careful choices when it comes to the best of their friends. Write the memory verse on a piece of paper and hang it on the fridge this week to help everyone in the family learn and remember it.

He who walks with wise men will be wise, but the companion of fools will suffer harm.
- Proverbs 13:20 NASB

Chapter 21 – Wise Man and Fool Cards

Wise Man: You get 10 points!

Wise Man: You get 10 points!

Wise Man: You get 10 points!

Wise Man: You get 10 points!

Wise Man: You get 10 points!

Wise Man: You get 10 points!

Foolish Man: You lose 20 points!

Foolish Man: You lose 20 points!

Chapter 22

Therefore go and make disciples of all nations.... – Matthew 28:19a

Theme:
We can share the good news of God with others.

Overview:
God wants us to tell everyone about Jesus and his love. He wants us to encourage them to grow closer and stronger with God.

Supplies:
- White coffee filters
- Washable markers
- Spray bottles, filled with water
- Paper towel or newspaper to protect the table

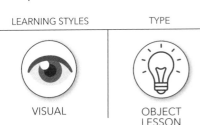

LEARNING STYLES	TYPE
VISUAL	OBJECT LESSON

Wrap-up: Just like in our little experiment, once the good news of Jesus starts to spread – there's no stopping it. That's because it's the best news ever. We can tell our friends and family all about the good news – the fact that God created us and wants a relationship with us. Even though we have fallen into sin, God has made a way for us to be saved – through the death of Jesus on the cross. This is really good news and definitely something worth sharing.

Activity 1

Spreading the Good News
(Coffee Filter Object Lesson)

Step #1: Give each child a coffee filter, washable marker, and piece of newspaper

Step #2: Instruct them to lay their coffee filter flat onto the newspaper.

Say: Jesus spent a lot of time with the disciples. He taught them and told them all about the kingdom of God. When Jesus was getting ready to return to heaven to be with his Father, he gave some instructions to the disciples. He wanted them to tell other people about him.

Step #3: Draw a circle with marker on the inside *(flat, un-ridged part)* of the coffee filter. Instruct the kids to do the same.

Say: Let's imagine that this circle of color is all the teachings of Jesus. Jesus didn't want them to just stay right here. He wanted them to spread to all the nations. Let's read our memory verse together *(read Matthew 28:19a from your Bible)*.

Step #4: Spray your coffee filter lightly with the spray bottle.

Say: So the disciples began to go out and spread the gospel. They started telling everyone they met about Jesus. Pretty soon, those people told other people, and the good news about Jesus spread and spread. We're not sure if there are disciples of Christ in all nations yet, but the more we tell others about Jesus, the closer we will get to that goal. Go ahead and spray your coffee filter *(lightly!)* and see how the good news of Jesus spreads.

Step #5: All kids to spray their coffee filters and observe how the color spreads to the ends of the coffee filters.

Bible Stories for This Activity
- Acts 2:37-47 Peters shares the good news and the Early Church grows
- Acts 9:20 Paul begins to share the good news with others

Activity 2

Ping Pong Toss Word Game

Step #1: Write the words of the verse on the note cards (ideally one word per card). Don't forget to include the reference.

Step #2: Tape the cards to the empty plastic containers. Set the containers up on a table or on the floor.

Say: Today, our memory verse comes from the book of Matthew. It was some of the last instructions Jesus gave to his disciples. He told them to go and make more disciples -- of all the nations. When you are a disciple of Christ, it means that you choose to follow him and obey his teachings. It's not just a one-time prayer – it's a decision to change how you live your life. Today, we're going to play a little game to help us learn the memory verse. Just like the disciples were to go out – you're going to send some ping pong balls out, and into these containers!

Step #4: *(Show the kids the containers with the words taped onto them.)*

Say: Let's say the verse together. When I hold up a container, you say the word written on it (Hold up the containers in order so kids can say the verse as a group).

Step #5: After you are done saying the verse, set the containers back on the floor or table. Pick a volunteer and have them stand about 1-2 feet from the containers (depending on their age).

Say: Okay, your job is to get a ping pong ball in every one of these containers in less than a minute. Ready?

Step #6: Hand the bucket of ping pong balls to the first player and set the timer for one minute (fun background music is a plus). Allow child to throw ping pong balls. When the minute is up, say the verse together as a group and then pick a new volunteer.

Wrap-up: It wasn't easy to get the ping pong balls in all the containers -- especially when you had only a minute to do it. It isn't easy to share the good news of Jesus with all the nations either. We can tell people about Jesus and pray for missionaries. Let's finish up praying for God to give us opportunities to share the good news with others.

Supplies:

- Ping pong balls (in a bucket)
- Several plastic containers with wide mouths (32 oz yogurt containers would work great)
- Note cards
- Tape
- Marker
- Timer

LEARNING STYLES	TYPE
KINESTHETIC	GAME

Bible Stories for Activities 2 and 3

- Romans 1:16 I am not ashamed of the Gospel
- John 3:16 God loved the world so much he sent Jesus to die for our sins
- Acts: Paul and his friends share the gospel with others
- Matthew 28:16-20 The Great Commission

Supplies:

- White construction paper
- Blue and Green crayons
- Children of the Nations figures from page 94
- Glue
- Scissors
- Poster of the memory verse (or write it on the board)

LEARNING STYLES	TYPE
LOGICAL	CRAFT

Make Disciples of All Nations Craft

Step #1: Make a copy of the Children of the Nations page for each child in your class

Step #2: Pass out a piece of white construction paper and a blue and green crayon to each child.

Say: Today's verse comes from the book of Matthew. This verse is a command that Jesus gave to his disciples and it is for us too. Let's read it together *(read from your Bible or from the poster)*. It says to make disciples of all nations. Today, we're going to make a craft that will help us to think about all the nations.

Step #3: Show the kids the page of children from around the world. Talk about what countries they might be from. Instruct kids to draw a picture of the earth in the middle of the construction paper (leaving room to glue the children around it later).

Step #4: When they are done with the earth, have them cut out the children of the nations and glue them around the earth.

Step #5: If there is room, write the day's memory verse on the page as well.

Wrap-up: This craft is a great way for us to remember Jesus's final command to his disciples. Did you know that we can tell others about God too? We might not be able to go to all the nations right now, but we can certainly pray for children in other nations and we can tell our friends and neighbors about God. Let's spend some time praying for children in other parts of the world now.

At-Home Activity

Hello! Today we talked about telling other people about God. Our verse comes from the book of Matthew (read it below) and it was one of the last things Jesus said to his disciples. Jesus told them to make disciples of all nations. In order to make a disciple, you have to tell someone about God and help them to grow in their faith. One of the best ways to grow in your faith is by attending church each week. My guess is that there are plenty of kids in your child's class that do not have a church home. Why not invite them to church with you sometime? It's exciting to know that we can obey Jesus's teachings and be part of this special mission.

Therefore go and make disciples of all nations…. – Matthew 28:19a

Chapter 22 - Children of the Nations

Chapter 23

Be kind to one another, tender-hearted, forgiving each other, just as God in Christ also has forgiven you.
  – Ephesians 4:32 NASB

Overview:
God was kind and loving to us by giving us a way to be forgiven through Christ. We should share that love and kindness with everyone around us.

Supplies:

- Piece of sturdy paper
- Small rock
- Tape
- Extra pieces of paper for children

LEARNING STYLES	TYPE
 VISUAL	OBJECT LESSON

Wrap-up: After saying the verse as a group, pass out paper to the group so they can practice making and flying their own paper airplanes. If possible, write the memory verse on the side of the plane so they will have something to practice later with.

Activity 1

Weighed Down by the Weight of Un-forgiveness

Step #1: Make a paper airplane out of your sturdy piece of paper.

Step #2: Gather children together and show them your airplane.

Say: Today, we're learning a verse from the book of Ephesians. This verse gives us instruction on how we should treat each other. Would someone like to read it for me? Let's imagine that this airplane is me. Usually, I'm pretty happy and soaring through life.

Step #3: Throw the airplane across the classroom. After it has landed, retrieve the airplane and hold it up for the kids to see again. Also hold up your small rock.

Say: Unfortunately, sometimes I get mad at people. Whenever that happens, I have a choice to make. I could forgive them, like God has forgiven me, or I could choose to stay angry. Sometimes we call this holding a grudge.

Step #4: Place the rock inside the top crevice of the plane. Tape the top together so it holds the rock inside.

Say: When we hang onto our anger, it really affects the way we live.

Step #5: Throw the plane again. Observe how it almost immediately crashes.

Say: Our anger drags us down. God doesn't want us to hold onto our anger. He wants us to forgive others, just as he has forgiven us. Let's say the verse together and then practice making our own paper airplane, free of anger and un-forgiveness.

Bible Stories for This Activity

- Colossians 3:12-13: Show kindness and love to each other
- Matthew 18:21-35: Parable of the unforgiving servant

Kindness Is Like Glitter

Step #1: Before class, prepare a poster of the memory verse. Use the liquid glue to trace over the word "kind". While the glue is still wet, sprinkle with glitter. Shake off excess.

Step #2: Show the kids the poster of the memory verse.
Say: Today, we're learning a verse from the book of Ephesians. Does anyone want to guess what word from this verse we're going to be focusing on? *(Allow kids to guess).* We're going to be talking about kindness. To help us understand kindness, I brought in a little something.

Step #3: Sprinkle some glitter on your hand.
Say: Kindness is a lot like this glitter. When you show kindness to someone, you spread the kindness.

Step #4: Shake hands with someone in the class. Observe how the "kindness" glitter has now spread to another person.
Say: Wow! Check it out. I showed kindness to my friend here and it spread onto their hands. I wonder what would happen if they showed kindness to someone else.

Step #5: Direct the first child to shake hands with another friend, spreading the "kindness" again.
Say: I think the glitter would just keep on spreading. That's the same way it is with kindness. When you show kindness to others, you brighten their day and they will probably show kindness to someone else in their life. What a great thing to put into practice. Now, we're going to make a craft to remind us to spread kindness like glitter.

Step #6: Pass out construction paper to the kids. Have them write "Be Kind" or "Kindness" in large letters on their paper. Trace over the letters with the liquid glue. While the glue is still wet, sprinkle glitter on top of the glue. Shake off the excess glitter. Along the bottom of the page, write the entire memory verse or the verse reference (whatever space permits).

Wrap-up: These are some dazzling works of art. I hope they remind you to show kindness throughout the week, just like our verse instructs us to. Let's practice the verse one more time together.

Supplies:

- Fine glitter
- Wet wipes (optional)
- Construction paper
- Marker or crayon
- Liquid glue
- Poster of the verse

LEARNING STYLES	TYPE
VISUAL	OBJECT LESSON

Bible Stories for Activities 2 and 3
- Colossians 3:12 Show each other kindness, compassion, and patience
- Galatians 5:22-23 Fruit of the Spirit
- Acts 9:36-42 Tabitha shows kindness by sewing clothes
- Ruth: Ruth shows kindness to Naomi and Boaz shows kindness to Ruth

Acts of Kindness Coloring and Check-Off Chart

Supplies:

- Construction paper
- Crayons
- Kindness chart found on 98 , one copy for each child
- Poster of the memory verse

LEARNING STYLES	TYPE
VISUAL	CRAFT

Step #1: Show the poster of the memory verse to the kids.

Say: Today, we are learning a verse from the book of Ephesians. This is a really helpful verse and something we can practice every single day. This verse instructs us to be kind and tenderhearted to others. What are some ways we can do this?

Step #2: Allow children to share ideas on ways to show kindness to others. You may want to use the chart on page 98 to give ideas if kids need some help getting started.

Say: Those are some great ideas! Let's draw some pictures of ways that we can show kindness to those around us.

Step #3: Pass out the construction paper and crayons to the kids and allow them some time to draw pictures. After everyone is finished, show them the kindness chart.

Say: You guys came up with some great ways to show kindness. Let's keep this attitude going all week long with this kindness chart. It has a bunch of ideas to show kindness to those around you. You each will take one home. Cross off or color in the squares as you complete the tasks and bring this back to me next week!

Wrap-up: Practice the verse together a few more times as a group. If time permits, hang up the pictures of acts of kindness.

At-Home Activity

Hello! Today, we took a closer look at a verse from Ephesians (you can read it below). This is a terrific verse for families to practice together. This week, brainstorm ways that you can show kindness to those around you. Specifically, think of ways that you can show kindness to:

- A neighbor
- A relative
- Someone who is old or young
- A leader in your community

After you have written down ways to show kindness, work together as a family to create a plan about when these acts of kindness will happen.

Be kind to one another, tender-hearted, forgiving each other, just as God in Christ also has forgiven you. – Ephesians 4:32

Chapter 23 - Kindness Chart

Smile or say hello to someone you don't know	Offer to carry something for someone	Write a nice note to your sibling	Help carry in the groceries
Tell a family member: I love you!	Get someone a drink	Sweep the kitchen floor	Draw a color a picture for your neighbor
Compliment a sibling	Give a parent a hug	Bake cookies for a neighbor or friend	Send a note to the police officers
Make a snack for a sibling	Invite a friend over to play	Tell a parent Something you like about them	Hold the door open for someone

Chapter 24

Come to me, all you who are weary and burdened, and I will give you rest.
— Matthew 11:28

Theme:
God will help us.

Overview:
When you are overwhelmed, tired, or upset, Jesus will help you. Pray to him and he will give you time to calm down and rest.

Supplies:

- White pillowcase, one for each student
- Fabric markers
- Smocks (optional)
- Poster of the verse
- White paper + crayons (optional)
- Stencils (optional)

LEARNING STYLES	TYPE
TACTILE	CRAFT

Tip:
You can find white pillow cases at discount stores for about $1-2 each.

Activity 1

I Will Give You Rest Pillowcase

Step #1: Give each child a white pillowcase and a few fabric markers. Show them the poster of the verse.

Say: Today, we're learning a verse about rest. Let me read it to you *(read from the poster or Bible)*. Do you ever feel weary or tired? *(Allow kids to answer)*. It's easy to get tired and worn out. Sometimes we just have too much to do! God tells us that he will help us by giving us strength and by taking away our worries. Today, we're going to make a craft to remind us to find rest in God.

Step #2: Encourage kids to copy the verse from the poster onto their pillowcase with the fabric markers. They may want to use the white paper and crayons to sketch out a design before coloring on the pillowcase.

Step #3: After they have copied the verse, encourage them to add more decorations to the pillowcase (maybe using stencils).

Wrap-up: When you take this pillowcase home, put it on your pillow on your bed. Before you go to sleep each night, say the verse out loud. Remind yourself that God will give you rest. If you are worried about something, pray about it and ask God to take away those burdens.

Bible Stories for This Activity

- Psalm 62:1-2 My soul finds rest in God alone
- 1 Peter 5:7 Casting all your cares on him, because he cares for you.

Activity 2

Pool Noodle Verse Stacking

Step #1: Prepare the pool noodles by writing the verse on the pieces. One word should go on each piece. Each color should have the complete verse written on it.

Step #2: Show the poster of the memory verse to the kids.

Say: Today, we are learning a verse from the book of Matthew. This is something that Jesus said to people while he was on earth. It applies to us as well. Jesus said that he will give us rest. Do you ever feel nervous or upset about something? Do you ever feel tired and weary? *(Allow kids to answer).* I think we all feel like that sometimes. Jesus tells us to talk to him about our troubles and he will give us rest.

Step #3: Show children the pieces of the pool noodle.

Say: We're going to have a little race to see who can put the words of the verse together the fastest.

Step #4: Demonstrate how to put the pool noodles on the dowel rod or broom stick *(you may need a partner to hold the rod for you)* so that when you are finished, you can read the verse in order. *(Kids may find it easier to start with the first word on the bottom and build up from there).*

Step #5: Pick two volunteers and give them each the pieces of one pool noodle. On your mark, have them race against each other to complete the verse. When they are finished, read the verse out loud as a group. Pick new volunteers as time permits.

Wrap-up: You guys did a great job putting the verse together today! This week, I want you to think about finding some quiet time to rest with Jesus. It might be right before bed or maybe when you are in the car. Talk with him and tell him about anything you are feeling weary or burdened about.

Supplies:

- 2 different colored pool noodles, cut into 3-4 inch pieces
- Permanent marker
- 2 large dowel rods or broom sticks
- Poster of the memory verse

LEARNING STYLES	TYPE	
KINESTHETIC	GAME	VERSATILE

Tip:
You can use an electric knife to easily cut a pool noodle.

Bonus:
Other kids can color the memory verse paper on page 102 while they wait for their turn.

Bible Stories for Activities 2 and 3

- Philippians 4:6-7 Do not be anxious, but rather pray
- Psalm 4:8 In peace I will lie down and sleep
- Psalm 23: The Lord is my shepherd and gives me rest
- Genesis 2:2-3 On the seventh day, God rested

Supplies:

- Soothing music and music player
- Battery operated candles
- Large floor pillows
- Calming story book about Jesus
- Paper and crayons (optional)
- Blankets (optional)

LEARNING STYLES		TYPE
KINESTHETIC	AUDITORY	ACTIVITY

Activity 3

Time of Refreshment

Step #1: Welcome kids into the classroom and have them sit near you.

Say: Today is going to be a different sort of day around here. Our verse today is all about finding rest in Jesus. So, we're going to do a little resting! Before we begin, let me read our verse to you (Read Matthew 11:28 from Bible). Is anyone feeling weary or tired today? *(Allow kids to answer).*

Step #2: Dim the light and turn on the battery operated candles. Have the kids help you spread out the floor pillows and have them pick a pillow to lay on.

Say: Go ahead and get comfortable. I am going to read you a story about Jesus and I want you to just lay and rest. Afterwards, we're going to spend a little time praying and talking to God about anything we feel burdened about or worried about.

Step #3: Read the story to the kids. Try to maintain an atmosphere of rest and calm.

Step #4: After the story is complete, encourage the kids to spend time praying silently. If kids would like to journal or color about their prayers, give them paper and crayons to work quietly. After a few minutes, pray out loud to wrap up the restful time.

Wrap-up: This was a wonderful time of rest. I hope you feel refreshed after this time. This week, I would encourage you to take time like this again to just sit and think about Jesus and to pray about anything that is troubling you.

At-Home Activity

Hello! Today, we learned a verse from the book of Matthew (you can read it below). It was something Jesus said to his followers and it is still important for us today. In this verse, Jesus promises that he will give rest to anyone who is feeling weary and burdened. Are you feeling that way this week? Take your cares to Jesus and ask him to refresh and renew you. Try to carve out some time this week to rest as a family (we know it's a challenge!). Perhaps you can do it through a family movie night or a Sunday afternoon nap. Whatever the method, try to take some time to rest and ask Jesus to help you with whatever burdens you may be facing. To help you remember the verse, write it on a note card and place it near the bed of each family member.

Come to me, all you who are weary and burdened, and I will give you rest.
– Matthew 11:28

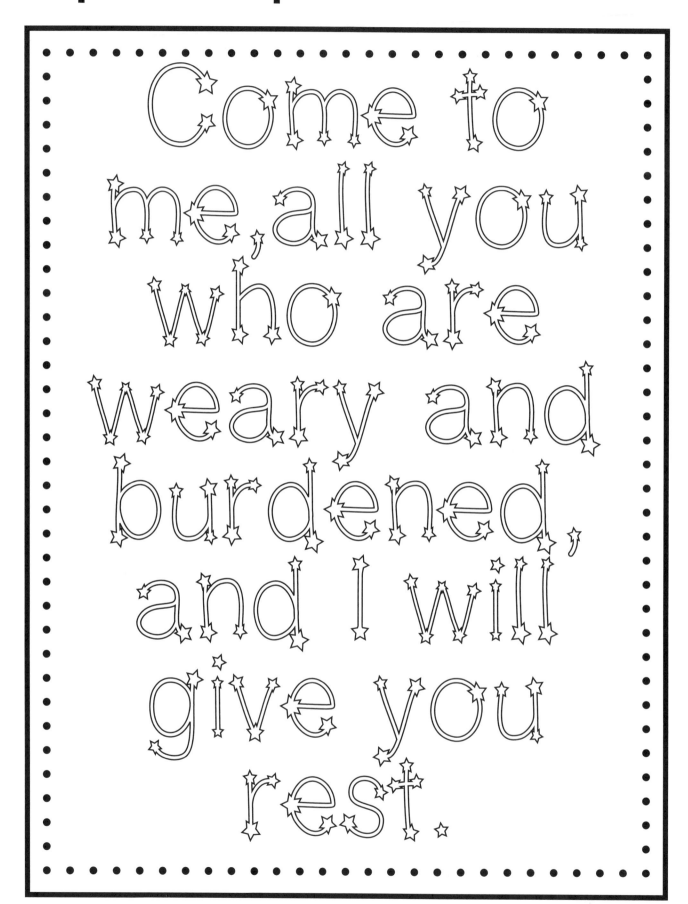

Come to me, all you who are weary and burdened, and I will give you rest.

Matthew 11:28

Chapter 25

Jesus wept. – John 11:35

Theme:
God cares when
we are sad.

Overview:
Jesus really loved and cared for those he spent time on the earth with. He loves you just as much. He cares when you hurt.

Supplies:
- Alphabet Stickers
- White paper
- Bibles
- Construction paper (optional)
- Glue (optional)

LEARNING STYLES		TYPE
VERBAL	TACTILE	CRAFT

Alternative Idea:
Can't find alphabet stickers? You can have kids cut letters out of old magazines and glue them onto the paper instead.

Activity 1

Sticker Alphabet Memory Verse

Step #1: Give each a child a Bible and help them to find John 11:35.

Say: Does anyone want to read the memory verse for today? *(Allow a volunteer to read).* It's pretty surprising how short the verse is! Even though it is short, it is important. This verse helps us to see how much Jesus cared for his friends *(Mary and Martha)* and how much he cares for us.

Step #2: Pass out a piece of white paper to each child. Spread out alphabet stickers on the table.

Say: We are going to make a poster of our verse today, using these stickers to spell the words of the verse.

Step #3: Allow the children to work on their posters, adding decorations with crayons or markers after the stickers are in place. Be sure to include the verse reference.

Wrap-up: Good job on the posters, everyone. Be sure to take this home and hang it up where you will see it this week. Let it remind you how much Jesus cares for you.

Bible Stories for This Activity
- Psalms 18:28 God turns darkness into light.
- Ephesians 5:7-14 Live as children of light.

Paper Plate Sadness to Gladness Craft

Step #1: Prepare a sample craft by drawing a sad face on one plate and a happy face on the other. Glue the two plates together (faces out) with a craft stick sandwiched in between the plates.

Step #2: Give each child two paper plates.

Say: Today, we've got a memory verse that I bet every single one of you could learn in under a minute. Do you want me to read it to you? *(Read John 11:35).* That's it. Pretty short, huh? Who would like to try and say the memory verse? *(Allow a few volunteers to say the verse).* Even though it is a very short verse, it's pretty important. This verse shows us how much Jesus cares about us. This happened when Jesus's friend Lazarus had died. Even though Jesus was about to raise Lazarus from the dead, he still felt bad that his friends were so sad. This is probably why he wept. The good news is that Lazarus did not stay dead. Jesus turned everyone's sadness into gladness.

Step #2: Show kids your sample craft.

Say: At first, the people were sad that Lazarus had died *(show the sad face side).* However, after Jesus raised him from the dead, they were all happy again *(show the happy face side).* You can make your own sad to glad craft to remind you of this story and our memory verse.

Step #3: Pass out crayons or markers and encourage kids to draw a happy face and sad face. If there is room, have them write the memory verse along the bottom of the sad face plate. Glue the plates together like the sample craft, sandwiching the craft stick in between.

Wrap-up: Isn't it great to know that Jesus cares about us? Sometimes it seems like God is not listening to our prayers. Mary and Martha might have felt like that when they asked Jesus to come and he did not come right away. However, everything worked out for God's glory. Even when it doesn't seem like God is helping, he is always right beside us and he cares about when we are sad.

Supplies:

- White paper plate (not Styrofoam), two per child
- Markers or crayons
- Glue
- Large craft sticks (one per child)
- Sample craft, pre-made

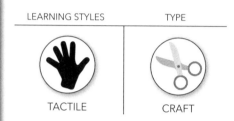

LEARNING STYLES	TYPE
TACTILE	CRAFT

Bible Stories for Activities 2 and 3

- John 11: Story of Lazarus
- 1 Peter 5:7 Casting all your cares on him, because he cares for you.
- Hebrews 5:7: Jesus prayed with tears
- Luke 19:41: Jesus wept over the city of Jerusalem

Supplies:

- White paper (cardstock or water color paper)
- Eye droppers (several for each child) or pipettes
- Liquid water colors or food coloring in water

LEARNING STYLES	TYPE
KINESTHETIC	CRAFT

Tip:

If you use watercolor paper, the paint will spread beautifully as the kids drop it onto the paper. Prepare the paper by brushing it lightly with water before dropping paint onto it.

** Make copies of the "Thinking of You" card template to send home with parents **

Activity 3

Water Dropper Paintings

Step #1: Pass out a piece of paper to each child. Distribute eye droppers and set the watercolors *(or water with food coloring)* where several children can reach them at once.

Say: Today's verse comes from the book of John. It is only two words. Does anyone want to guess about the words? *(Allow children to guess).*

Step #2: After children are down guessing, read to them John 11:35.

Say: This verse is found in the story of Lazarus dying. You may have heard the story before. Lazarus was sick and his sisters asked Jesus to come. Jesus did not come right away and by the time he arrived, Lazarus was dead. Everyone was so sad and even Jesus cried. Jesus probably cried because he knew his friends were so sad. This story had a surprising ending – Lazarus did not stay dead. Instead, Jesus raised him from the dead. Today, we're going to make a craft that will remind us of Jesus's tears.

Step #3: Demonstrate to the kids how to suck up a bit of color into their eye dropper or pipette. Drop the color onto the paper, just like a tear would fall from an eye. Observe how the color spreads and mixes with other colors if you drop them near each other.

Step #4: Allow children to work on their art projects, setting them somewhere safe to dry once they are finished.

Wrap-up: These are some beautiful pieces of art. Isn't it interesting to know that Jesus feels sad just like us at times? God made us and he understands all our emotions – happy and sad. Whenever you are feeling upset, you can talk to God about it. He cares about you no matter what you are feeling.

At-Home Activity

Hello! Today, we learned a verse from the book of John (you can read it below). This verse is found during the account of Lazarus's death and resurrection. Even though Jesus knew that he was about to raise Lazarus from the dead (read all about it in John 11), he still was sad for his friends. Just like Jesus showed compassion and love for his friends, we can show compassion and love for the people in our lives. Using the card provided, think about someone you know who might be sad or hurting. Write them a note of encouragement and send it their way.

Jesus wept. – John 11:35

Chapter 25 - Thinking of You Card

Chapter 26

Take delight in the Lord, and he will give you the desires of your heart.
– Psalm 37:4

Overview:

God loves us very much and wants to give us the desires of our heart. When we delight in God, our desires naturally begin to line up with God's will for our lives.

Supplies:

- Sticky notes
- Wall to hang notes on
- Markers or colored pencils

LEARNING STYLES	TYPE
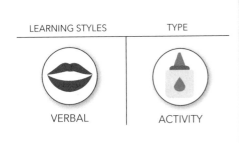	
VERBAL	ACTIVITY

Activity 1

Delighting in God
(Time of Praise)

Step #1: Introduction

Say: In our verse today, we are instructed to delight in the Lord. When we take delight in something or someone, it means that person or thing gives us great pleasure. There are many wonderful things about our God. Today, we're going to think about the things that make us happy when we think about God. We will write them down and then we will spend some time praising God for all his delightful attributes.

Step #2: Give each child 2 sticky notes. Instruct them to write down something that they find delightful about God. It could be something that he has done, a prayer he answered, a characteristic *(such as being all-powerful),* or a way that he has comforted their heart.

Step #3: When everyone is done, have them place their sticky notes on the designated wall. Gather everyone together.

Say: These notes are great. Isn't it amazing all the ways we can take delight in the Lord? Right now, we're going to spend some time in prayer. I'm going to tap your shoulder, one at a time, and when I do – I want you to pray to God and praise him for the things you wrote on your sticky notes.

Step #4: Spend a few moments in prayer, allowing each child to praise God for the things they wrote.

Wrap-up: Our memory verse today says that when we delight in the Lord, he will give us the desires our heart. The most important thing in our life should be our relationship with God. When that happens, everything else falls into place.

Bible Stories for This Activity

- Psalm 106:1 Give thanks to the Lord
- Matthew 6:33 Seek first the Kingdom of God
- Ruth: She chose to follow God and God gave her a new husband and child

Activity 2

Heart Jump
Memory Verse Game

Step #1: Using the heart template from Chapter 2, make hearts from various colors of construction paper. You will need between 15-20 hearts.

Step #2: Write the words of the memory verse on the hearts. You may want to write 2 of the smaller words on a few hearts. Place hearts in order on the floor. Optional: Secure to the floor with masking tape.

Step #3: Gather kids up near the hearts. Have them take off their shoes.

> **Say:** Our memory verse today says that when we delight in the Lord, he will give us the desires of our hearts. To delight in the Lord means that God makes us happy. When we put God first, he brings blessings to our lives. The memory verse is written in these hearts. We're going to jump from heart to heart, saying the verse out loud to help us memorize it.

Step #4: Demonstrate to kids how to jump from heart to heart (in order), saying the verse as you go. Allow the kids to jump after you, one at a time, saying the verse out loud. After everyone has gone through the hearts once, flip one of the hearts over so the word is hidden *(or cover up with a piece of construction paper).*

> **Say:** Okay, it's going to get a little harder now. Let's see if you can jump through the hearts again, with one of the words of the verse hidden. Do you remember the word? Let's give it a try.

Step #5: Allow the kids to jump through the hearts again, trying to remember the hidden word. Continue flipping or hiding a word for each round until the kids can say the verse completely on their own.

Wrap-up: Way to go, everyone! I hope you had fun jumping through this verse. God loves us very much and wants to give us the desires of our heart. When we delight in God, our desires naturally begin to line up with God's will for our lives. Let's pray and ask God to help us love him more and find delight in him.

Supplies:

- Heart Template from Chapter 2
- Construction paper in various colors
- Scissors
- Masking tape (optional)
- Extra construction paper (optional)

LEARNING STYLES	TYPE
KINESTHETIC	GAME

** Could be used with other heart-themed or love-themed verses. **

Bible Stories for Activities 2 and 3

- James 1:17 Every good gift is from God
- 1-2 Samuel: David delighted in the Lord, and God made him king
- Luke 10:42: Mary chose to delight in the Lord
- Jeremiah 29:13 You will find me when you seek with all your hear

Supplies:

- Small pom-poms, preferably in pink, red, and white colors
- Liquid glue
- Psalm 27:4 Template sheet on page 110
- Sample craft (optional)

LEARNING STYLES	TYPE
TACTILE	CRAFT

Warm Fuzzy Heart Art Project

Step #1: Make a copy of the Psalm 27 sheet on page 110 for each child. You may want to copy onto cardstock for extra stability.

Step #2: Give each child a handful of pom-poms, the Psalm 27 page, and some liquid glue.

Say: Our verse today is all about delighting in the Lord. The Bible tells us that when we delight in the Lord, he will give us the desires of our heart. Today, we're going to work on a project that helps us learn our verse.

Step #3: Instruct kids to place glue inside the heart on the page and then stick the pom-poms in the glue, filling in the heart. If they want, they could glue pompons around the edge of the paper as well.

Wrap-up: When everyone is finished, have them hold up their works of art and show the class. Practice the verse together as a group several times.

At-Home Activity

Hello! Today in class, we learned about delighting in the Lord. You can continue to learn and practice the memory verse with your child(ren) this week (find it below). Here is a fun game you can play as a family to practice delighting in the Lord.

Cut a piece of printer paper or construction paper into strips. Write one or two words of the verse on each strip and then staple them together to form a chain. Hang the chain from a door frame in your home. Each day, say the verse using the chain to help if needed. After saying the verse as a family, cut one of the chains away. Do this each day until you can say the verse without any help.

Take delight in the Lord, and he will give you the desires of your heart.
- Psalm 37:4

Take delight in the Lord,
and he will give you the
desires of your heart.
Psalm 37:4

Chapter 27

Do not merely listen to the word, and so deceive yourselves. Do what it says.
– James 1:22

Theme:
God wants us to read and obey the Bible.

Overview:
We should listen to what the Bible says and live it out in our lives.

Supplies:

- White paper or cardstock
- Crayons
- James 1:22 Ear page on page114

LEARNING STYLES	TYPE
TACTILE	CRAFT

Activity 1

Listen and Do Art Project

Step #1: Make a copy of the James 1:22 ear page for each child. Pass out crayons.

Say: Our memory verse today has some instruction for us. It explains that we should not merely listen to God's Word *(the Bible)*, we should also do what it says. It's much easier to just listen to the Bible and not change anything about our lives, but that's not how God wants us to live. Today, we're going to do a project that will remind us to listen to the Bible and do what it says.

Step #2: Instruct kids to draw a self-portrait face in the space between the ears. They may want to add clothes or earrings as well.

Step #3: Display the pictures for everyone to see and have kids try to guess who drew which picture.
Wrap up: These are some great art projects! I hope they remind us to both listen to and obey God's Word. Let's say the memory verse all together.

Bible Stories for This Activity

- 1 Samuel 3:15-21 Samuel heard from God and acted on the message
- Matthew 13: Parable of the Seeds and the Sower

Activity 2

Listen Up Game

Step #1: Gather kids together in a group. Have them spread out at least arms length apart.

Say: Our verse today comes from the book of James. It says that we should not only listen to God's Word (the Bible), we should also do what it says. It reminded me of the game called: Simon Says. The things written in the Bible help us a live a holy life, but the instructions in this game will just be for fun.

Step #2: Pick a leader and allow them to give commands to the kids for about 1 minute. Remind the kids that they should only obey the leader if they say "Simon Says" before the command. If kids do not obey "Simon" or if they obey without the "Simon Says" preface, they should sit down till the end of the round.

Step #3: After the first minute is up, pick a different leader and play again. Play 3-5 rounds as time permits.

Say: You guys did a great job listening to the instructions and doing what they said. It's not always so easy with the Bible. What are some things in the Bible that are difficult to do? *(Allow answers).* The Bible helps us live a life that is pleasing and glorifying to God – but only if we do what it says.

Wrap-up: Let's finish up by saying our memory verse together *(Hold up poster)* and then praying that God will help us listen to the Bible and do what it says.

Supplies:

• Poster of the verse

LEARNING STYLES		TYPE
VERBAL	KINESTHETIC	GAME

Bible Stories for Activities 2 and 3

• Judges: The Israelites knew the commands of God
• Matthew 7: A wise man is the one who hears the word of God
• Matthew 12:50: Whoever does the will of the Father is my brother, mother...
• Luke 11:28: Blessed are they that hear the word of God and obey it.

Supplies:

- Child-appropriate magazines with plenty of large words
- Glue sticks
- Scissors
- Poster of the verse, or verse written on board
- White printer paper or construction paper
- Laminator and laminating sheets (optional)

LEARNING STYLES	TYPE	
TACTILE	CRAFT	VERSATILE

Magazine Word Memory Verse

Step #1: Lay out the magazines within easy reach of the kids. Give each child a pair of scissors and a glue stick.

Say: Our verse today comes from the book of James. Let's all say it together *(hold up the poster if needed)*. What do you think is easier? Listening to the Bible or doing what it says? *(Allow answers)*. God wants us to both listen to his Word and to obey it *(do what it says)*. Today, we're going to make a project to help us memorize our verse.

Step #2: Instruct kids to look for large words in the magazines. They need to find all the words that are in the verse. Cut out the words from the magazine and glue them in order onto the page. If time is running short and they cannot find all the words, they can draw in the missing words with markers or crayons.

Step #3: If time permits, laminate the finished posters for extra durability.

Wrap-up: When everyone is finished, have them hold up their works of art and show the class. Practice the verse together as a group several times.

At-Home Activity

Hello! Today in class, we learned about listening and obeying God's Word, the Bible. You can continue to learn and practice the memory verse with your child(ren) this week (find it below).

Here's a fun game you can play as a family to learn the verse together. Write the verse on a piece of paper so family members can see it if needed. Pass around the paper and have each person read (or say) the verse in a funny or different voice. Here are some ideas to get you started:

- Whisper the verse
- Say the verse slow
- Say the verse in a sing-songy voice
- Clap the syllables in the verse

- Say the verse fast
- Pinch your nose and say the verse
- Say the verse, pretending you are dizzy
- Say the verse in a pirate voice

Do not merely listen to the word, and so deceive yourselves. Do what it says. - James 1:22

Chapter 27 - James 1:22 Listen

Do not merely listen...
Do what it says.
James 1:22

Chapter 28

Dear friends, let us love one another, for love comes from God.
— 1 John 4:7a

Theme:
God wants us to love each other

Overview:
When we loves others the way God loves us, they learn about God's love and will want to have it in their lives.

Supplies:

- Watercolor set (one per child) with brush
- Cups of water
- Love stencil on page 118 (letters cut out to create stencil)
- Printer paper or watercolor paper
- Smocks (optional)

LEARNING STYLES	TYPE
TACTILE	CRAFT

Activity 1

Watercolor Love Stencil

Step #1: Create several stencils by copying page 118. You will need one stencil for each child.

Step #2: Pass out stencils, paper, watercolors and cups of water to the kids.

> **Say:** Today, our verse is all about love. Let me read it to you *(Read the first part of 1 John 4:7 to the kids)*. Our verse tells us to love others just as God has loved us. It's not always easy to love others, but the closer we are to God, the more our love for others will grow. Right now, we're going to make a project to remind us of the importance of loving others.

Step #3: Demonstrate how to lay the Love stencil on top of the white paper. Encourage kids to paint each letter a different color. After the entire word is painted, remove the stencil to reveal the watercolor letters.

Wrap-up: Very nice work here! I hope this simple word will remind you of how much God loves you and how he loves for us to love each other. Let's say the verse one more time together.

Bible Stories for This Activity

- John 13:34-35: Love one another as God has loved you
- Romans 12:10: Be devoted to one another in love. Honor one another above yourselves.

Activity 2

Up and Down Verse

Step #1: Introduction

Say: Today our memory verse comes from the book of 1 John. Let me read it to you. *(Read the first part of the verse to the kids from your Bible).* This is a great verse for us because it gives us some really clear instructions *(love one another),* and it also tells us that love comes from God. It's not always easy to love others. Sometimes we get frustrated or angry with others. However, we can choose to love them and be kind even when it is hard because love comes from God. God can put love in our hearts so that we can show love to others.

Step #2: Have all the kids sit in the chairs. Explain that you are going to read the verse slowly *(use the version above).* They should stand up and sit down with every other word. For example:

> Dear - Stand
>
> friends, - Sit
>
> let -Stand
>
> us - Sit
>
> love –Stand

Step #3: Encourage the kids to say the verse along with you if they are able.

Step #4: After reading through the verse once, read it again, speeding up your reading a bit. Continue in the pattern until it is clear that the kids cannot keep up with the speed.

Wrap up: Whew! What a work out! That was some good sitting and standing. Does anyone think they can say the verse all by themselves? *(Allow kids to say verse).* I'm impressed with all your memory verse work today. Let's say the verse together one more time!

Supplies:

• Chairs

LEARNING STYLES	TYPE
KINESTHETIC	ACTIVITY

Bible Stories for Activities 2 and 3

• John 15:9 As the Father has loved me, so have I loved you.
• 1 John 4:19 We love because he [God] first loved us
• Luke 6:35 Love your enemies
• Mark 12:31 Love your neighbor

Supplies:

- Large white poster board (one for every 5 kids)
- Markers
- Red and pink washable paint
- Heart shaped cookie cutters (ideally one per child)
- Smocks
- Paper plates
- Poster of the 1 John 4:7a (or write it on the board)

** Could be used with any love themed verse **

LEARNING STYLES	TYPE	
TACTILE	CRAFT	VERSATILE

Heart Stamped Memory Verse Poster

Step #1: Gather kids into groups of 4-5. Give each group a poster board and have them put on smocks.

Step #2: Pour a small amount of pink paint and red paint on the paper plates *(just enough to dip the cookie cutters in)*.

Say: Our verse today comes from the book of 1 John. Would anyone like to read it from their Bible? *(Allow a child to read 1 John 4:7)*. We're going to be concentrating on the first part of the verse. We're going to make an art project as a team to help us learn the verse today.

Step #2: Give kids markers and instruct them to write the memory verse *(copying from the poster or their Bibles)* in the middle of the poster board. After the verse is written, kids can add hearts all around it by dipping cookie cutters in the paint and then pushing them onto the poster board.

Step #3: When kids are finished, have them rinse off the cookie cutters and remove their smocks.

Wrap-up: These are some amazing works of art. When they are dry, I will hang them up around the room and they can remind us to love others just as God loves us.

Make a copy of the reproducible from Chapter 9 to send home with families. Consider offering a prize when kids return the chart filled in.

At-Home Activity

Hello! Today in class, we learned a verse about love. You can continue to practice the memory verse with your child(ren) this week. Grab the page with small hearts on it. (If you forget to grab one – just make your own by drawing 12 hearts on a page). Look for ways to show love to others. Examples might include:

- Leaving a bottle of water for the postal worker.
- Helping someone in your family clean up their room.
- Talk to the person in front of you in line. Compliment something about them.
- Offer to babysit for someone who might need a break.
- Color a picture for someone who is sick or sad.

Each time you show love to others, write a brief description in the heart and color it in. When all the hearts are filled in, return it to your child's teacher.

Dear friends, let us love one another, for love comes from God. – 1 John 4:7a

Chapter 28 - Love Stencil

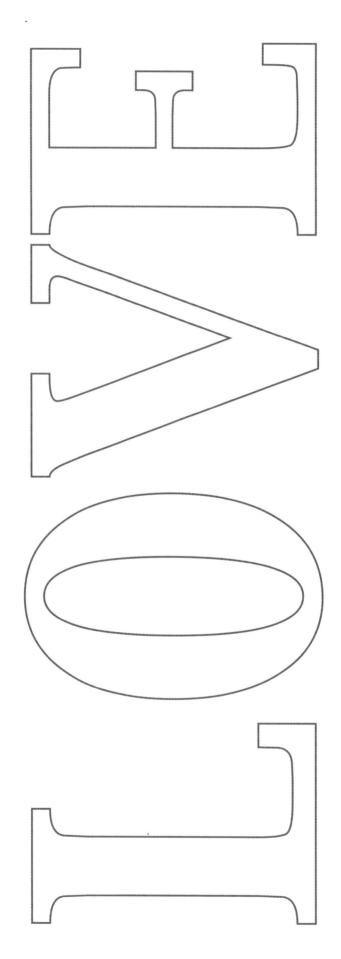

Chapter 29

But the fruit of the Spirit is love, joy, peace, forbearance, kindness, goodness, faithfulness, gentleness and self-control. Against such things there is no law.
– Galatians 5:22-23

Theme:
God's Spirit helps us to follow God's commands

Overview:
When we love God and follow his ways, people can see the changes in us. Our actions and attitude change and produce fruit.

Supplies:

- Fruits of the Spirit Memory Matching Cards on page 122 (one sets for each child)
- Scissors

LEARNING STYLES	TYPE
VISUAL	GAME

Activity 1

Memory Matching Cards

Step #1: Introduction

Say: Today our memory verse comes from the book of Galatians. This was one of the letters written by Paul, the apostle. It was written to the church in Galatia and it gives instructions on how we should live as Christians. When we become a follower of Jesus *(also known as a Christian)*, the Holy Spirit comes and lives inside of us. The Holy Spirit gives us power to obey God's commands. The more we listen to the Holy Spirit, the more we will show the fruits of the Spirit in our lives. There are many fruits of the Spirit. Let me read the verses to you (Read Galatians 5:22-23 from your Bible). Which one do you think is the easiest? *(Allow answers).* Which one do you think is the hardest? *(Allow answers)*

Step #2: Pair kids up and give each child a copy of the memory matching cards on page 122. Have them cut the cards apart on the black line and lay them out on the table face down.

Step #3: Instruct kids to take turns flipping two cards over to try and get a match. Whoever has the most matches at the end of the game *(when all the cards are gone),* wins. If kids finish early, encourage them to put the fruits of the Spirit in order, according to the memory verse.

Wrap-up: Nice job pairing up those fruits of the Spirit, everyone! Let's lay out your cards face up on the table. As we say the verse together, touch the correct fruit as we say it. *(Repeat the memory verse together as a group one or two times).*

Bible Stories for This Activity

- Colossians 3:12-17 Put on kindness, humility, meekness, patience…
- John 15:5 I am the vine, you are the branches

Activity 2

Fruit of the Spirit Tree

Step #1: Pass out white construction paper to each child. Instruct them to draw the trunk of a tree and branches as you introduce the verse for the day (*you may want to prepare a sample craft for them to look at for reference*).

Step #2: Introduce the Bible verse

Say: Today, our verse is all about the fruits of the Spirit. Has anyone ever heard of these before? Do you know any of the fruits of the Spirit (*Allow answers*). Just like a tree grows fruit, we can grow a type of fruit in our life. What kind of fruit would an apple tree grow? (*Allow answers*). That's right -- apples. (*Continue to name a few other fruit trees*) In the same way, a Christian will grow Christian fruit. We call this the fruit of the Spirit, because it is the Holy Spirit that helps it grow inside of us. Let me read to you what the fruits of the Spirit are (*Read Galatians 5:22-23 from your Bible*). Today, we're going to make a tree and hang these "fruits" on it to remind us of our memory verse.

Step #3: After kids are done drawing and coloring in their tree trunks and branches, pass out various colors of construction paper. Instruct kids to cut out circles from the construction paper. Each child should have 9 different circles.

Step #4: After the circles are cut out, instruct the children to write the fruits of the Spirit inside the circles (*one fruit per circle*). If they need help remembering, have them look up their verse in their Bibles.

Step #5: Glue the "fruit" circles onto the tree branches. Kids may wish to fill in the trees with leaves using a green crayon. Write the verse reference (*Galatians 5:22-23*) at the bottom of the page.

Wrap-up: I love these fruit trees! I am so glad that the Holy Spirit gives us the power to grow all these fruits in our lives. I'm sure I could not do it on my own. I hope these lovely works of art will help you learn and remember our memory verse this week.

Supplies:

- White construction paper
- Brown crayons or markers
- Circle hole puncher (optional)
- Various colors of construction paper
- Glue
- Pen, pencil, or black fine tip marker
- Sample craft (optional)
- Green crayons (optional)

LEARNING STYLES	TYPE
TACTILE	CRAFT

Tip:
If you are not using the circle hole puncher, you may want to provide simple circle stencils or have some pre-cut circles for the younger ones.

Bible Stories for Activities 2 and 3

- John 15:16: God appointed you to bear fruit
- Philippians 1:11: Fruit of righteousness
- Matthew 12:33: You will know a tree by its fruit
- Colossians 1:10: Bear fruit of good work

Fruit Toss

Supplies:

- Orange
- Poster of the verse

   ** Could be used with other verses as well. Just substitute the orange for a small ball.**

LEARNING STYLES	TYPE	
KINESTHETIC	GAME	VERSATILE

Step #1: Gather kids up and have them sit in a circle.

Step #2: Show the orange to the kids.

Say: Can anyone tell me what this is? *(Allow answers)*. Yes, it is an orange. An orange is the fruit that an orange tree produces. Did you know that the Bible says we should produce fruit in our life as well? It's not fruit like apples and oranges. Rather, it is called the fruit of the Spirit because it is the Holy Spirit that helps it grow in our lives. Let me read to you what the fruit of the spirit is *(Read from your Bible or the poster)*. Today, we're going to play a little game to help us learn our memory verse.

Step #2: Pass the orange to one of the kids. Instruct the kids to say the verse in a steady rhythm with you *(they may want to clap in rhythm to help keep the beat)*. With each syllable, the kids should pass the orange to the player on their right.

Step #3: The orange will continue to pass, one kid per syllable, until you reach the end of the verse. Whoever is holding the orange when the verse ends go inside the circle. They can continue to clap, but they will not be passing the orange.

Step #4: Hand the orange to another player and continue the game till there is only one player left. Play again as time allows.

Wrap-up: That was a lot of fun passing that orange around. I hope next time you see an orange you remember that Christians should grow fruit in our lives as well - the fruits of the Spirit. Does anyone want to try and say the verse on their own? *(Allow kids to say the verse as time allows)*.

At-Home Activity

Hello! Today in class, we learned a verse all about the fruits of the Spirit. It's a pretty long list (see verse below), but thankfully, we don't have to do all these things by our own strength. God has promised that his Holy Spirit will produce these fruits in us. The closer we get to God, the more we will see these fruits of the Spirit in our lives. This week, spend some time praying as a family, asking God to help these "fruits" grow inside of your lives.

But the fruit of the Spirit is love, joy, peace, forbearance, kindness, goodness, faithfulness, gentleness and self-control. Against such things there is no law.
- Galatians 5:22-23

Chapter 29 – Fruit of the Spirit Memory Cards

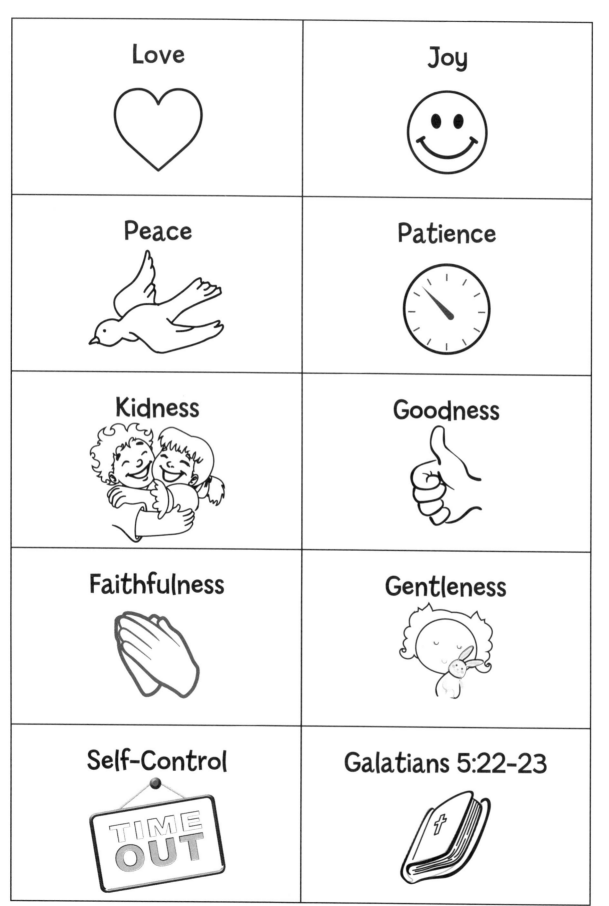

Love

Joy

Peace

Patience

Kidness

Goodness

Faithfulness

Gentleness

Self-Control

Galatians 5:22-23

Chapter 30

All Scripture is God-breathed and is useful for teaching, rebuking, correcting and training in righteousness. – 2 Timothy 3:16

Theme:
God's Word (the Bible) teaches us the right way to live.

Overview:
All Scripture comes from God, helps us correct our bad choices, helps us be better people, and grow closer to him.

Supplies:
- Construction paper
- Large tip marker
- Timer
- Tape
- Large wall

LEARNING STYLES	TYPE	
KINESTHETIC	GAME	VERSATILE

Activity 1

Tap the Page
(Memory Verse Letter Game)

Step #1: Introduction

Say: Today our memory verse comes from the book of 2 Timothy. It tells us about God's Word, the Bible. This verse tells us that all Scripture comes from God *(is God-breathed)* and it is useful for teaching, rebuking *(reprimanding or scolding)*, correcting, and training. That's a lot of stuff! The Bible is full of wisdom and encouragement. It helps us know the right path to choose and it gives correction if we start to stray from that path. Today, we're going to play a game to help us learn and memorize this verse.

Step #2: Tape 15 pieces of paper to a wall. Spread them out so they are about a foot apart. On each paper, write the first letter of each of the words of the verse. For example, the first few papers should have the letters "A", "S", "I", and "G" on them for "All Scripture is God-breathed".

Step #3: Line kids up near the first piece of paper. Have them touch each piece of paper as they say the corresponding word of the verse. Allow the entire group to practice going through the verse a few times and then time each kid (you may want to shorten the verse for younger players) to see who can say the verse (correctly!) the fastest.

Wrap up: Pretty impressive work, guys! I loved how quickly you were able to learn this very important verse from the Bible. Let's say the whole thing one more time as a group to finish up our game.

Bible Stories for This Activity

- Hebrews 4:12: The Word of God is living and active
- Romans 15:4: Scripture was written for our instruction

Activity 2

What's Missing Memory Verse?

Step #1: Begin by writing the memory verse onto note cards, one word per card.

Step #2: Ask for a volunteer. Have them sit in the chair, facing a wall. Blindfold the volunteer.

Step #3: Place the note cards in order on the floor near the blindfolded volunteer. Pick another volunteer to quietly sneak up and steal one of the words. They should return to their seat and hide the note card.

Step #4: After the "thief" has returned to their seat and hidden the card, take the blindfold off the original volunteer. Allow them to look at the verse, reading it out loud and trying to fill in the missing word. If they say the verse correctly, they can try to guess who stole the word (allow them 2-3 guesses). After they have finished guessing, reveal the thief and choose a new volunteer to be blindfolded.

Step #5: Replace the stolen word and chose a new "thief" to steal a different word. Continue playing in this way as time allows.

Wrap-up: You guys did a great job swiping those memory verse words and remembering the verse even with the word missing. Nice work! All the words in this verse are important. They tell us that Scripture comes from God (is God-breathed) and the words tell us what Scripture is good for. Does anyone remember the four things? (Allow answers). Very good! Scripture is good for teaching, rebuking, correcting and training in righteousness. I would encourage you to keep working on this verse throughout the week.

Supplies:

- Note cards
- Marker
- Chair
- Blindfold

LEARNING STYLES	TYPE	
VISUAL	GAME	VERSATILE

Bible Stories for Activities 2 and 3
- Psalm 119:105 Your Word is a lamp unto my feet
- Matthew 4 Jesus rebukes Satan with Scripture

Memory Verse Motions Poster

Supplies:

- Camera
- Sign language book or access to ASLpro.com
- Poster board
- Marker

LEARNING STYLES | TYPE

VISUAL | ACTIVITY

Turn to page 126 for another great activity.

Step #1: Write the words of the verse on a poster board, leaving enough spacing to glue pictures above the words later.

Step #2: Read the verse to the kids.

Say: Today, we are learning a verse from the book of 2 Timothy. This verse is packed with helpful information about Scripture. It tells us that God's Word, the Bible is God-breathed – which means it comes from God. It also tells us that the Bible is helpful for teaching, rebuking, correcting, and training in righteousness. We're going to come up with some motions today to help us learn the verse.

Step #2: Using the sign language book or website as inspiration, come up with motions for each word/phrase in the verse. Take pictures of several kids doing these motions.

Step #3: Practice the verse several times as a group doing the motions.

Step #4: After class, get the pictures developed and glue them onto the appropriate spaces on the poster. Next week, show the completed poster to the kids and practice the verse again as review.

Wrap-up: Nice work coming up with motions! I'll get these pictures developed for next week and then we can check out the completed poster!

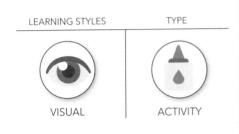

At-Home Activity

Hello! Today in class, we learned a verse from 2 Timothy 3:16 (read it below). Scripture (the Bible) is useful for all kinds of things including teaching us the right way to live life. Of course, the Bible cannot help us with these things (teaching, correcting, training) if we do not take the time to read it. This week, spend some time as a family reading God's Word together. You can read from a kid's Bible or a regular Bible. The important thing is to begin building the habit of reading the Bible regularly. Aim for about 5 minutes each day. You may want to read a few of your favorite accounts, or just pick a book and read through chapter each day. Talk about what kinds of things you are learning from Scripture as you read and how the verse can help you live life God's way.

All Scripture is God-breathed and is useful for teaching, rebuking, correcting and training in righteousness. – 2 Timothy 3:16

The Bible Is God's Words

Coded Message: Use the key found below to decipher the message from 2 Timothy 3:16

___ _____ __ ___

_____ ___ __ ___

_____ ___ __ _____

___ _____ _____

_____ ___ _____

__ _____ ___ _____

__ _____.

A = ↳	I = ⇥	R = ↻
B = ⇄	J = ⇈	S = ᆺ
C = ⇶	K = ⇊	T = ⌃
D = ⇆	L = ∩	U = ⌰
E = ↥	M = ℧	V = ‿
F = ⇶	N = ↰	W = ‿
G = ⇟	O = ↺	Y = ⇞
H = ⇇	P = ↻	Z = ⇐

Chapter 31

I have hidden your word in my heart that I might not sin against you.
– Psalm 119:11

Theme:
God's Word (the Bible) teaches us the right way to live.

Overview:
When we memorize God's Word, the Holy Spirit is able use it to help us not make bad choices.

Supplies:

- Heart hole puncher (or copies of the small hearts from Chapter 9, page 42)
- Construction paper
- Glue
- Scissors (if not using heart hole puncher)

** Could be used with any heart/love themed Bible verse **

LEARNING STYLES		TYPE
TACTILE	VERSATILE	CRAFT

Activity 1

Hide God's Word in My Heart Art Project

Step #1: Begin by having kids write the memory verse in the middle of a piece of construction paper.

Step #2: Allow kids to use the heart hole puncher to cut out hearts from various colors of construction paper. If you have a large group, you may wish to punch out some ahead of time. If you choose to use the small hearts page - have kids color in the hearts and then cut them out.

Step #3: Glue the hearts all around the outside of the edge of the paper, creating a fun and festive frame for the memory verse.

Step #4: Have kids hold up their finished works of art and practice saying the verse a few times together as a group.

Wrap-up: You guys did a great job making these works of art. Be sure to hang it up somewhere where it will remind you to hide God's Word in your heart.

Bible Stories for This Activity

- Psalm 119:105 Your Word is a lamp unto my feet
- 2 Timothy 3:16 All Scripture is God-breathed and useful for…

Hide the Bible Game

Step #1: Introduction

Say: Today our memory verse comes from the book of Psalms. This chapter in Psalms was written by King David and this verse shows us how important Scripture was to King David. Our verse tells us that David hid God's Word in his heart *(memorized God's Word)* in order to keep himself from doing the wrong thing. The more we learn and memorize Scripture, the easier it is for us to know right from wrong. Hiding God's Word in our hearts *(memorizing the Bible)* helps to keep sin out of our lives.

Step #2: Show the kids the Bible

Say: Of course, David didn't mean he literally hid God's Word *(the Bible)*. It is just an expression. But in this game, we are indeed, going to hide the Bible.

Step #3: Select one volunteer and give them the Bible. Have the rest of the group face a wall and cover their eyes while the volunteer hides the Bible.

Step #4: After God's Word is successfully hidden, have kids remove their hands from their eyes. Say the memory verse together as a group and then let the kids search for the Bible. Whoever finds the Bible first can hide it next. Remember to say the verse as a group before each round of hiding and finding.

Wrap up: That was a fun game, but that's not exactly what David meant when he wrote this verse. When we hide God's Word in our hearts, it means we memorize verses or parts of the Bible. It is "hidden in our hearts" because it is always with us. No one can take it away from us and we will always be able to remember it when we need it. Has anyone here hidden a part of God's Word in their hearts? *(Allow answers)*. I would encourage you to keep on hiding God's Word in your hearts whenever you can. Let's finish up by saying our verse together.

Supplies:

- Bible
- Large playing area

LEARNING STYLES	TYPE
KINESTHETIC	GAME

Bible Stories for Activities 2 and 3

- Hebrews 4:12: The Word of God is living and active
- Romans 15:4: Scripture was written for our instruction
- Psalm 37:31: The law of God is in his heart, he does not slip.
- Colossians 3:16: Let the Word of God dwell in you.

Supplies:

- Stop that Sin Activity Page on page 130
- Bibles (one for each child or each team)
- Markers, crayons, or pencils

LEARNING STYLES	TYPE	
LOGICAL	PUZZLE	ACTIVITY

Stop that Sin!

Step #1: Make a copy of the activity page for each child or team of kids. Give each child/group a Bible.

Step #2: Read the verse to the kids from your Bible.

Say: Today, we are learning a verse from the book of Psalms. This verse was written by King David and it gives us a bit of a battle plan against sin. It tells us that God's Word, when we memorize it and make it a part of our life *(hide it in our hearts)* will keep us from sin. Today, we're going to look at a few verses and see how they would give us direction in our life and help us steer clear of sin.

Step #2: Allow kids to look up the verses in their Bible and then draw lines to the corresponding sin that the verses would help us fight against.

Step #3: When everyone is done, go over the answers as a group.

Step #4: Practice the memory verse a few times as a group.

Wrap-up: Nice work coming up with matching up these verses. Can you see how hiding God's Word in your heart would help you not to sin? What is a favorite verse of yours? *(Allow answers).*

At-Home Activity

Hello! Today in class, we learned a verse from Psalms. This memory verse tells that we can hide God's Word in our hearts. When we read and memorize the Bible, we hide it in our hearts. This week, why not play a hiding game as a family?

Write the memory verse (find it below) on a note card and hide it somewhere where a family member would unexpectedly find it (in a lunch box, under a pillow, taped to the milk). When someone finds it, it is their job to hide it again. Keep hiding and finding the memory verse all week long.

I have hidden your word in my heart that I might not sin against you.
- Psalm 119:11

Chapter 31 - Stop That Sin

I don't want to forgive my brother for breaking my toy	**Colossians 3:13**
I'm not that bad. I don't have sin in my life, really	**Romans 3:23**
I know I have a lot of clothes I could give to someone in need, but I just don't want to.	**James 4:17**
I broke one my mom's favorite figurines. I don't want to get into trouble, so I hid it	**Proverbs 28:13**
Some kids at school were so mean to me yesterday. Today, I'm really going to get them back!	**Romans 12:17**
Sometimes my sister really bothers me. I just want to yell at her and make her go away!	**Ephesians 4:32**
I can figure out things for myself. I don't need God's help	**Proverbs 3:5-6**
I do like God, but there are things in my life I like a lot more. Like my video games.	**Matthew 22:37**
Sometimes my parents have the most ridiculous rules. Does God really want me to obey all the time?	**Colossians 3:20**
Do I really have to love my neighbor? They didn't do anything nice for me.	**1 John 4:19**

Chapter 32

If we confess our sins, he is faithful and just and will forgive us our sins and purify us from all unrighteousness.
– 1 John 1:9

Theme:
God forgives our sins.

Overview:
God promises to forgive us our sins when we are truly sorry and ask for forgiveness. To forgive us means he erases them as though they never happened.

Supplies:

- Chalkboard or dry erase board
- Chalk or dry erase markers
- Quiet, contemplative music (optional)

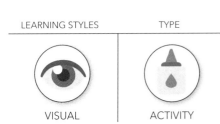

LEARNING STYLES	TYPE
VISUAL	ACTIVITY

Activity 1

God Will Forgive and Erase Your Sins

Say: Today, we're going to be learning a verse from 1 John 1:9. *(Read verse from your Bible)*. This verse promises that God will forgive our sins when we confess them. Even though I try to do the right thing, I still make mistakes. Do you ever do the wrong thing or make mistakes?

Step #1: Allow kids to answer the question, one at a time. As they give answers, write them on the board.

Say: It looks like we all make mistakes and sin. In fact, the Bible tells us that everyone sins. Thankfully, we don't have to get stuck in our sin. Right now, we're going to spend some time praying to God and confessing our sins to him. You can pray to God and he will forgive you. You can pray in your head or out loud. I'll give you a few minutes and then I'll tell you when time is up.

Step #2: Play some quiet, contemplative music (optional) and dim the lights if possible. Allow kids to spend some time in prayer, confessing their sins. As they pray *(hopefully with their eyes closed),* quietly erase the board.

Step #3: After 2-3 minutes, quietly tell the kids that prayer time is finishing up. Invite them to end their prayer time and open their eyes.

Say: Look what happened to our sins? They were erased. The same thing happens to the sin in our lives when we confess our sins to God. Our verse today tells us that God is faithful to forgives us and purify us. That's some seriously good news!

Wrap-up: I'm so glad that God will forgive our sins when we confess our sins. Let's read or say the memory verse together again.

Bible Stories for This Activity

- Psalm 32:5 I confessed my sins and you forgave me
- Proverbs 28:13 Whoever hides his sins will not prosper…

Get Rid of that Sin
(Sock Game)

Step #1: Split kids up into two teams and place them on either side of the dividing line. Dump out an equal number of socks on each side of the line.

Say: Today our memory verse comes from the book of 1 John. It tells us that if we confess our sins, God is faithful to forgive our sins. That means he takes them away. However, in this game, you're going to spend a lot of time trying to get rid of your "sin".

Step #2: Hold up one of the rolled up socks to show the kids. **Say:** In this game, we're going to pretend that this sock symbolizes sin. You are going to try your best to throw all your sins to the other side of the line. Of course, the other team will be doing the same thing, so it's going to be a bit crazy. I'm going to set the timer for one minute. Whoever has the most "sins" on their side of line when the timer beeps loses the round.

Step #3: Set the timer and let the kids begin throwing the socks. When one minute is up, have all kids sit down as you count up the socks. Declare a winner. Play again as time permits.

Wrap-up: That was a fun game, but I sure am glad that we don't actually have to try to get rid of our sins this way. Let's read our verse for today *(read 1 John 1:9 from your Bible)*. This verse tells us that if we confess our sins, God is faithful to forgive us and purify us. That's certainly good news, and a whole lot easier than trying to throw all these socks!

Supplies:

- Rolled up socks (optimally between 20-30 socks)
- Dividing line
- Large playing area
- Timer

LEARNING STYLES	TYPE
KINESTHETIC	GAME

Bible Stories for Activities 2 and 3

- Acts 3:19 Repent and turn to God so your sins may be forgiven.
- Daniel 9:9 The Lord is merciful and forgiving
- Jeremiah 29:12 When you call on me, I will hear you
- Psalm 17:6 Hear my plea, LORD

Whisper Your Sin Game

Supplies:
• None

LEARNING STYLES | TYPE

AUDITORY | GAME

Step #1: Have kids sit together in a circle.

Step #2: Read 1 John 1:9 to the kids from your Bible.

Say: This verse contains some really good news. We all make mistakes at times. We all sin. The good news is, though, that we don't have to keep carrying that sin around with us. If we confess our sin, God will forgive us. It seems almost too good to be true, but God loves us and wants to get rid of the sin in our lives. I love that we can talk directly to God. In the Old Testament, the people had to offer sacrifices and talk to a priest in order to receive forgiveness. We don't have to do that anymore. We can talk directly to God and he can forgive us.

Step #3: Introduce the game

Say: In this game, we're going to see what might happen if we had to pass a message through several people.

Step #4: Whisper a short sentence to one child. Have them whisper it to the next child in the circle. Repeat this process until the message has gone all the way around the circle. Have the final child say the message out loud. If the results are typical, the message will be very different than the one you originally whispered.

Say: That's just crazy! Can you imagine what might happen if we had to pray like this? What if we had to tell our sins and requests to a whole chain of people instead of talking to God directly? I'm so glad that we can pray straight to God. We can confess our sins and talk to him about anything.

Wrap-up: Read the verse again to the children, and then play the whispering game a few more times.

At-Home Activity

Hello! Today in class, we learned a verse from 1 John 1:9. In this verse, we are assured that God will forgive our sins if we confess and repent. It's not always easy admitting our mistakes, but it's much better to confess than to continue to carry the burden of sin around with us.

This week, it might be a great idea to model some confession to your children. Did you make a mistake this week? Did you do something that you knew was wrong? Say these things out loud and spend time in prayer, showing your children what it means to confess our sins to God.

If we confess our sins, he is faithful and just and will forgive us our sins and purify us from all unrighteousness. - 1 John 1:9

IF WE CONFESS OUR SINS, HE IS FAITHFUL AND WILL FORGIVE US OUR SINS AND CLEANSE US FROM ALL UNRIGHTEOUSNESS.

1 John 1:9

134

Chapter 33

Let everything that has breath praise the LORD. Praise the LORD.
— Psalm 150:6

Theme:
We were created to give glory to God.

Overview:
If we have breath, we should be praising God for all he is and does for us. Even the animals praise God.

Supplies:

- Music player
- Children's ministry praise songs
- Simple musical Instruments (egg shakers, maracas, tambourines, jingle bells, etc)

LEARNING STYLES		TYPE
AUDITORY	MUSIC	ACTIVITY

Tip:
If you do not have simple musical instruments, see Activity #2 to learn how to make some.

Song Suggestions:
- Hosanna Rock
- Every Move I Make
- Let Everything That Has Breath

Activity 1

Let's Praise the Lord

Step #1: Introduction

Say: Today, we're going to be learning a verse from the book of Psalms. The verses that are written in the Psalms are mostly either songs or poems. Let's see what our verse says today. *(Read Psalm 150:6 from your Bible)*. This verse tells us that everything that breathes *(or has breath)* should praise the Lord. Do you have breath? What about me? *(Allow answers)*. So, it seems like we should be doing some praising!

Step #2: Pass out musical instruments.

Say: We're going to spend a little time praising God. One way that we can praise God is by singing and making music. I'm going to play a song. If you know it, sing along. If you don't know it yet, go ahead and make some music with your instruments.

Step #3: Play a simple praise song for the kids to listen to and sing along with. If kids are very young, they may enjoy going on a "Parade of Praise", walking around the room and using their musical instruments as they listen to the song.

Step #4: Once the song is over, gather kids around you.

Say: How did it feel to praise God in that way? There are many ways we can praise God. What are some other ways we might praise God? *(Allow answers)*.

Wrap-up: God is amazing! We can let him know how much we love him by spending time praising him each day.

Bible Stories for This Activity

- Psalm 149:3 I will praise God with music and dancing
- Psalm 71:23 I will sing for joy

Simple Musical Instruments

Step #1: Split kids up into groups, depending on which musical instrument they would like to make.

Say: Today our memory verse comes from the book of Psalms. Let's read it together. *(Read Psalm 150:6 from your Bible).* This verse tells us that we should all be praising God. Sounds like a lot of fun to me! Let's work on making some musical instruments and then we'll spend some time praising with shouts and music.

To make the Balloon Bongo drum: Cut the nozzle off the balloon and stretch the bottom part over the top of a clean tin can. Tape balloon in place. Repeat with a second balloon. Play the drums with hands or plastic spoons.

To make the Egg Shakers: Fill a plastic egg with beans or rice (or a combination). Close egg and tape shut with washi tape to seal.

To make a Jingle Bell Stick: Glue a large jingle bell to the end of a craft stick.

To make Water Bottle Maraca: Fill water bottle with small objects. Replace lid and screw tightly. Cut paper towel lengthwise and begin to fold it in on itself. Place it on the lid of the water bottle and squeeze roll until it is tight against the lid. Tape in place. Continue to tape all the way down the paper towel roll to create a sturdy handle for the maraca.

Wrap up: Once all the musical instruments are completed, play some simple upbeat music and have the kids play their instruments along with the music. Encourage them to say things like "Praise God!", "Thank You God!" or other expressions of praise.

Supplies:

For Balloon Bongo Drums:
- Clean tin can
- Balloons
- Rubber band or packing tape

For Egg Shakers:
- Plastic dggs
- Washi tape
- Rice or beans

For Jingle Bell Sticks:
- Large jingle bells
- Low temp hot glue gun
- Large craft sticks

For Water Bottle Maracas:
- 8 oz empty water bottle
- Small objects to fill up bottle (small erasers, beads, beans, screws, pasta, seeds, etc)
- Paper towel roll
- Electrical tape

LEARNING STYLES		TYPE

TACTILE	AUDITORY	CRAFT

Bible Stories for Activities 2 and 3
- Acts 3:19 Repent and turn to God so your sins may be forgiven.
- Daniel 9:9 The Lord is merciful and forgiving
- 1 Chronicles 16:25 Great is the Lord and greatly to be praised
- Revelation 4:11 Worthy are you Lord, to receive glory

Praise God Puzzle

Supplies:

- Copy of Praise God puzzle on page 138 (one for each child or team of kids)
- Pencils
- Bibles

LEARNING STYLES	TYPE
LOGICAL	PUZZLE

Step #1: Pass out the puzzle to the kids along with a Bible. You may want to pair kids up in teams. Read Psalm 150:6 from your Bible to the group.

Say: Our verse today that everything that has breath should praise the Lord. We have many reasons to praise God. In this puzzle, you'll discover some reasons to and some ways to praise God.

Step #2: Allow kids to work on the puzzle, helping when needed.

Wrap-up: Read the verse again to the children and spend some time talking about things we can praise God about.

At-Home Activity

Hello! Today in class, we talked about Psalm 150:6 (read it below). There are many reasons to praise God, but often, we get so busy in daily living that we forgot about the blessings that God has given us. This week, you are encouraged to set up a "Praise Wall" somewhere in your home.

Make sticky notes available and encourage each family to write something they are grateful for or something they are praising God for. Continue this practice each day. At the end of the week, read through all the blessings and praise, taking time to pray and thank God for all he has done.

Let everything that has breath praise the LORD. Praise the LORD.
- Psalm 150:6

Chapter 33 - Praise God Puzzle

Let everything that has breath praise the LORD. Praise the LORD.

Psalm 150:6

Chapter 34

To act justly and to love mercy and to walk humbly with your God.
— Micah 6:8

Theme:
The Bible tells us how to live.

Overview:
We share the love of God when we show mercy to people.

Supplies:

- Various ingredients for a trail mix (pretzels, popcorn, nuts, dried fruit, candy, etc.
- Small measuring cups
- Small plastic zippered bags
- Situation of Justice cards on page 142

LEARNING STYLES	TYPE
TACTILE	FOOD

Warning:
Avoid nut items to protect against allergies.

Wrap-up: It's not always easy to act justly in our daily lives. Often we want the best or the biggest thing for ourselves. However, that is not how God wants us to act. You can be a light to the people around you when you seek to act justly and do the right thing.

Activity 1

Justice Trail Mix

Step #1: Introduction

Say: Have you ever heard of the word "justice"? What do you think it means? When have you heard it used? *(Allow answers)*. In our Bible verse today, the prophet Micah told the people they should act justly. To act justly means that we understand there is a clear right and wrong – and we strive to do the right thing.

Step #2: Discuss situations of justice *(using the reproducible page 142)*

Say: Being just doesn't always mean that everyone gets the same thing, but it does mean that people get what they need. What do you think justice would look like in these situations? *(Allow some discussion)*

Step #3: Divide the room into two groups. Give one group the ingredients for the trail mix *(each child or pair of children get one ingredient)* along with a small measuring cup *(1/8 cup or similar)*. Give the other group the small zippered bags *(one per child)*. Allow the children with bags to go down the line and receive each ingredient for their trail mix.

Step #4: Have the second group *(the ones with their plastic bags now filled with trail mix)* hold their bags up.

Say: Does everyone have the same amount of each ingredient in their bag? *(Allow answers)*. I don't think so, but each child does indeed have some trail mix. Being just doesn't always mean that everyone gets the same thing.

Step #5: Allow kids to switch places so the everyone has a chance to fill a bag.

Bible Stories for This Activity

- Colossians 3:12 Act with kindness and meekness
- Proverbs 21:3 Justice and righteousness is better than sacrifice

Love Mercy Watercolor Pictures

Step #1: Introduction

Say: Who can tell me what mercy means? *(Allow kids to answer)* The dictionary tells us that mercy means showing kindness or forgiveness to an offender or enemy. That is not easy to do! Have you ever shown mercy to someone who has hurt you? *(Allow kids to answer)*

Step #2: Pass out a piece of paper and markers to the kids. Encourage them to draw a picture of someone showing mercy, kindness, or forgiveness. When they are drawing, encourage them to not color in picture, but leave it as mostly line art.

Step #3: After they are done with the markers, pass out watercolors and water to the kids. Have them fill in the pictures with the watercolors. The markers will not bleed with the water and it will create a nice effect for their artwork.

Step #4: When everyone is finished and the pictures are dry, hang them up on the wall. Label them with a sign that says "We Can Show Mercy" along with the Bible verse.

Wrap-up: It's not always easy to show kindness or mercy to an enemy. Often, when someone is mean to us, we want to get back at them. This is not how Jesus acted though, and it is not how we should act as Christians. Even when Jesus was being mocked, spit on, and beaten before he was crucified, he did not retaliate or attack his enemies. It's not an easy task, but God will give us the strength to do it.

Supplies:

- Permanent markers
- Watercolor paints with brushes
- White paper or watercolor paper
- Small cups of water

LEARNING STYLES	TYPE
TACTILE	CRAFT

Alternative idea:
Have kids use watercolors to paint in the reproducible found on page 134.

Bible Stories for Activities 2 and 3

- 1 Peter 2:23 Jesus did not retaliate
- Colossians 3:13 Forgive one another
- Colossians 2:6-7 Continue to live your lives rooted in Christ
- Psalm 1:2 But they delight in the law of the LORD, meditating on it day and night.

Supplies:

- Beans
- Straws
- Bowls
- Table
- Timer, set to 1 minute

LEARNING STYLES	TYPE
KINESTHETIC	GAME

Wrap-up: It was hard work getting each bean into that bowl, but slowly and surely, you began to get quite a collection of beans. The same is true with our walk with God. Each day takes a little work. We cannot develop a deep relationship all in one day, but as we walk with him each day (through prayer and reading the Bible), we will deepen our relationship with God slowly and surely.

Walking Humbly with God (Bean Relay)

Step #1: Get game ready by placing beans in the middle of the table *(directly onto the table)*. Place a bowl on each end of the table.

Step #2: Introduction

Say: Our Bible verse for today gives us some instructions for living. Would anyone like to read Micah 6:8 for me? *(Allow a child to read verse or read it yourself)*. One of the things this verse instructs us to do is to walk humbly with God. The closer we grow to God, the more we realize how amazing he is. This causes us to be humble because we are able to see what an incredible gift it is to have a relationship with Christ. Of course, like so many things, a deep relationship with God does not happen all at once. It happens slowly and a little bit at a time – kind of like the game we are going to play.

Step #3: Choose two children to be the first players in the game. Give each child a straw and have them stand near the pile of beans.

Say: I'm going to start the timer and you will have 1 minute to pick up as many beans as possible. You will have to grab the beans by sucking through the straw. The goal is to pick it up off the table and put it in your bowl. Whoever has the most beans at the end of the minute wins.

Step #4: Start the timer and encourage the rest of the kids to cheer their friends on. When they are done, count up the beans and declare a winner. Say the memory verse all together as a group. Select two more players and continue game as time permits.

At-Home Activity

Hello! Our verse for today gives us some very good instructions for living. When we act justly, we look out for others who may be in need. When we love mercy, we show forgiveness and kindness to our enemies. When we walk humbly with God, we make it a priority to develop our relationship with him. As a parent (or grandparent), which part of this verse is most difficult for you? What do you find the easiest? Spend some time this week and talk as a family about this verse. Was there a time that you acted justly or showed mercy? Share that story with your children. Is there something you are currently doing that is developing your relationship with God? Share that practice with your children. Brainstorm ways you can live out this verse in your life this week.

To act justly and to love mercy and to walk humbly with your God. - Micah 6:8

Chapter 34 - Situation of Justice cards

What Does Justice Look Like?

What would you do to see justice done in the following situations?

You have plenty of clothes in your closet, but you know your cousin is in need of some clothes.

Your family has enough to eat, but you know someone in your church who is having a hard time with money.

You have been using the swing for a long time at the playground, and you can see there are other kids waiting.

It seems like certain kids at school get picked on or teased more than others.

There's a classmate who would like to play with you, but you don't usually include her because she's not "your favorite friend".

You're going on a family bike ride and it's hard for the youngest child to keep up with the rest of the group.

You're in an art class making pictures of flowers. There is only one purple crayon. You really want to make a field full of purple flowers, but you heard some other kids say they would like to make purple flowers too.

There's someone in your class that doesn't speak English very well. They have only been in America for a short time. You notice that she often gets left out at recess because it's hard for others to understand her.

Chapter 35

Give thanks to the LORD, for he is good.
His love endures forever.
– Psalm 136:1

Theme:
God is good.

Overview:
We should always be looking for ways
to give God our thanks.

Supplies:

- Poster of Psalm 136:1
- Large area where kids can spread out a bit

LEARNING STYLES	TYPE

AUDITORY

GAME

VERSATILE

Tip:
You could make this game a little more high-tech by recording the kids ahead of time with a voice recorder or an app on your phone. Just be sure to keep track of who is on each track!

Activity 1

Who's Saying the Verse?

Step #1: Have kids sit down in a circle on the floor, at least one arms-width apart from each other.

Say: Today's verse is from the book of Psalms. We're going to play a guessing game to see if you can guess who is saying/reading the verse. To begin, I want you all to close your eyes and cover them with your hands. I'm going to tap the shoulder of one child who will quietly open their eyes and stand up.

Step #2: Tap the shoulder of one child and quietly lead them away from the group. Have them read or say the verse out loud from a distance. When they are done reading, have them quietly return to the group and cover their eyes again.

Step #3: Once the verse-reader is back into place, allow everyone to uncover their eyes. Have kids raise their hands to take a guess at who said the verse, allowing 3 guesses per turn. Once they have guessed (*or you have revealed the reader*), have everyone cover their eyes again and repeat the process.

Wrap-up: What a crazy way to practice the memory verse. Sometimes it was easy to guess and sometimes it was really tough! You guys did a great job reading and saying the verse. Let's say it as a group one more time.

Bible Stories for This Activity

- 1 Chronicles 16:34 Give thank to the Lord for he is good
- Psalm 145:9 The Lord is good to all, and his mercy is over all that he has made.

Activity 2

Gratitude Memory Game

Step #1: Pass out the note cards to the kids along with a few colored pencils or markers. Let kids know they are welcome to trade and share the coloring utensils.

> **Say:** Today's verse comes from the book of Psalms. Psalms is a collection of songs and poems. Many of the Psalms were written by David, but there were a few other authors as well. In this verse, the author is praising God for his goodness and his love. Right now, we're going to do the same thing.

Step #2: Open your Bible and read Psalm 136:1 to the kids.

> **Say:** We can give thanks to God for many things. On two of your note cards, I want you to write something that you are grateful for. It can be something like a favorite food, a place you like to visit, or something that you enjoy doing *(like going for a bike ride or giving someone a hug).*

Step #3: Allow kids time to write down something they are grateful for, helping them with spelling if they need it. Once they have written on two of their cards, have them draw coordinating pictures on the remaining two cards (for example, if a child wrote "my cat" on one card, have them draw a picture of their cat on another card, creating a pair of cards).

Step #4: Once the pictures are completed, go around the room and have each child hold up their cards in pairs, telling the group what they are praising God for. Once everyone has shared their cards, mix them up in a big pile and play a game of memory (concentration) together. If you have a large group, divide kids up into groups of 5 to keep the game moving along.

Wrap-up: Isn't it amazing all the good things that God has provided for us? I'm glad that we can take a moment to thank God for his goodness and love!

Supplies:

- Note cards, enough for each child to have 4
- Colored pencils or markers

LEARNING STYLES	TYPE
VISUAL	GAME

grateful

Bible Stories for Activities 2 and 3

- Psalm 118:1 Give thanks to the Lord, for he is good…
- Psalm 106:1 Praise the Lord… for he is good…
- Psalm 9:1 I will give thanks to you, Lord, with all my heart…
- Psalm 95:2-3 Let us come before him with Thanksgiving

Supplies:

- Camera
- Ladder
- Large space for kids to lay down on

LEARNING STYLES	TYPE
KINESTHETIC	ACTIVITY

Human Thanks

Step #1: Introduce the verse.

Say: Today, we're taking a closer look at Psalm 136:1. Would someone like to read that from the Bible?

Step #2: Allow a child to read the verse or read it to the group yourself.

Say: The key word we're going to focus on today from this verse is "Thanks". You are going to work together as a group to spell out the word "Thanks" using your bodies. When you are all arranged, I'll take a picture standing on this ladder.

Step #3: Help kids arrange themselves so they spell out "Thanks" with their bodies. If there are more kids than needed, have the extra kids form a frame around the word. When they are all in place, take a few pictures from the top of the ladder. Have the kids say the verse while in position.

Step #4: During the week, get the picture developed (one copy for each child) and write the memory verse on the back for them.

Wrap-up: Nice work guys! That was a complicated way to say thanks! I'm glad that we don't have to work that hard to praise God for his goodness and love. Let's spend a few minutes praying, thanking God for the good things he has brought into our lives.

At-Home Activity

Hello! Our verse today is all about giving thanks to God. You can give thanks to the Lord as a family by playing this fun alphabet themed game (great for car rides!). Begin with the letter "A" and name something that you are thankful to the Lord for. The next person in the family will name something they are grateful for that starts with the letter "B." Work your way all through way through the alphabet, praising God for his goodness. To add another level of difficulty, try to see if you can remember all the things that were named before your turn.

Give thanks to the LORD, for he is good. His love endures forever.
- Psalm 136:1

GIVE THANKS TO THE LORD, FOR HE IS GOOD. HIS LOVE ENDURES FOREVER.

Psalm 136:1

146

Chapter 36

Do to others as you would have them do to you.   - Luke 6:31

Theme:
God wants us to be kind to others.

Overview:
When we treat others like we want to be treated we show the love of God to them.

Supplies:
- Poster board
- Markers
- Sticky tac or tape to hang chart on wall

LEARNING STYLES	TYPE
VISUAL	ACTIVITY

Wrap-up: When we read the Bible, we learn right and wrong, and we learn how to make good decisions. Just like a candle or torch would help us find the path in the dark words, God's Word helps us choose the right path in life.

Activity 1

Picture of Kindness

Step #1: Introduce the verse.

Say: Today's verse comes from the book of Luke. Luke was written by someone who was friends with Jesus and this verse is something that Jesus said. Jesus told his followers that they should treat others the way they wanted to be treated. How do you usually want to be treated? *(Allow children to answer, leading them toward saying "with kindness").* Usually, we like to be treated with kindness, so that is how we should treat others. We're going to work together as a group to make a "picture of kindness", thinking about ways we can use our whole bodies to show kindness to others.

Step #2: Draw a person figure on the poster board, leaving room on each side to add notes.

Step #3: Point to the eyes on the person you drew.
Say: Let's think about our eyes. How can we use our eyes to show kindness to others? *(Allow answers).* Those are great answers. We can use our eyes to watch for someone who might be sitting alone or feeling sad. We can use our eyes to look at someone else. Sometimes something as simple as making eye contact can help a person feel special.

Step #4: As the kids give answers, write them down on the poster near the eyes. When they have given a few ideas, move onto another part of the body, such as the mouth.
Say: What about the mouth? How can we use our mouth to show kindness to others? *(Allow kids to answer, writing down their answers as they say them.)*

Step #5: Continue in this way until your poster is filled up. At the bottom of the poster, write the memory verse (Luke 6:31).

Bible Stories for This Activity
- Matthew 22:39 Love your neighbor as yourself
- Galatians 5:14 The law is fulfilled in…. love your neighbor as yourself

Activity 2

Good Samaritan

Step #1: Prepare the name tags.
Write the following on the name tags (one person per tag): Jewish man, Samaritan, Priest, Levite, Innkeeper, Robber

Step #2: Gather the children together.
Say: Today our Bible verse may be one that you have heard before. It comes from the book of Luke. Would anyone like to read Luke 6:31? *(Allow a child to read verse or read it yourself)*. It's not always easy to treat someone the way we want to be treated. Sometimes we would rather be selfish or do what we want to do. But that is not the best way to live. We're going to look at a story from the Bible today where a few people did not obey this verse, while one man did. See if you can figure out who treated others the way he would like to be treated. Read Luke 10:25-37 to the kids.

Step #3: After finishing reading the story, ask a few questions:
• Who do you think treated the hurt man the way he would want to be treated?
• Why do you think the other two men did not stop?
• Have you ever seen someone who needs help but chose not to help them? Why?

Step #4: Introduce the skit.
Say: I'm going to read through the story again, but this time, you are going to act out the parable along with me.

Step #5: Pass out the name tags to the kids and have them put on simple Bible robes. If there are not enough parts for all the of the kids, have the extra kids sit along the wall to be the audience. Read through the passage again, allowing children to act along with the story.

Wrap-up: It's not always easy to follow this verse, is it? What are some reasons that we do not treat others well? (Allow answers). Let's say our memory verse together as a group a few times and then pray that God will give us the opportunity to treat others the way we would like to be treated this week.

Supplies:

• Bible (may want to use Children's Bible)
• Simple Bible robes
• Bandages or strips of fabric
• Gold coins
• Name tags and marker

LEARNING STYLES	TYPE
KINESTHETIC	GAME

Bible Stories for Activities 2 and 3

• Luke 5:17-26 Friends bring a paralyzed man to Jesus
• 1 Samuel 25:2-42 David and Nabel interact
• Ruth and Naomi - Ruth showed her mother in law kindness
• 2 Samuel 21: David was kind to Jonathon's son, Mephibosheth

Supplies:

- Cones, one for each team
- Large area to run
- Copy page 150 "Run this way" cards, cut along the lines (each child will need one card)

LEARNING STYLES   TYPE

KINESTHETIC   GAME   VERSATILE

Step by Step Memory Verse Race

Step #1: Set up race area. Divide kids into teams of 4-5 and set up cones to show the beginning and end of the race area. Explain to kids that they will run, relay race style to the cone at the end of the race area, run around the cone and return to their team to tag the next person in line.

Say: This is no ordinary relay race, though. You will have to run according the card you receive. And with each step that you take, you must say one word of the verse, including the reference.

Step #2: Pass out the cards to the kids, making sure each kid receives one card and they understand how to follow their card in the race.

Step #3: Practice the verse out loud with the kids two or three times before the race begins. When it seems like kids have a pretty good grasp on the verse, have them line up behind their starting cones.

Step #4: Start the race, making sure kids are saying the verse along the way. When a team member has run the race, have them sit down so you can easily see when a team is complete. When the race is finished, declare a winner. Play again if time permits, having kids switch their "run this way" cards.

Wrap-up: When we read the Bible, we learn right and wrong, and we learn how to make good decisions. Just like a candle or torch would help us find the path in the dark woods, God's Word helps us choose the right path in life.

At-Home Activity

Today, we talked about the verse commonly known as "The Golden Rule". While it's a pretty easy verse to memorize, it certainly isn't always easy to put into practice! This week, practice showing kindness to others in fun and unexpected ways.

Here are some ideas to get you started:
- Let someone go ahead of you in line
- Get someone a drink of water without being asked
- Put a bag of food in the car to give away to a homeless person when you see them
- Make a "thinking of you card" and mail it to someone
- Leave a note of encouragement in a library book
- Give a friend or family member a hug

Write out the memory verse and hang it near your door so you can see it as you come in and out each day.

Do to others as you would have them do to you.   - Luke 6:31

Chapter 36 - Run This Way cards

Run this way! Run like a....

Bear, with your arms up like giant claws	Monster, roaring and trying to scare people
Elephant, stomping loud and swinging your trunk	Fancy person, hands on your hips and waving like royalty
Mouse, with teeny tiny steps	Kangaroo, with giant hops
Horse, galloping at great speed	Hyena, laughing louder with each step
Crab, skipping sideways as you go	Eagle with arms spread wide and soaring in the sky
Turtle, walking slow and steady	

Chapter 37

He is not here; he has risen,
just as he said. – Matthew 28:6a

Theme:
Jesus is stronger
than death.

Overview:
Our Savior is alive! There is nothing more
powerful than him, not even death.

Supplies:
- Poster of the Matthew 28:6a
- Large area where kids can spread out a bit
- Soft ball for kids to toss

LEARNING STYLES		TYPE
KINESTHETIC	GAME	VERSATILE

Activity 1

Toss the Ball, Say the Verse

Step #1: Arrange kids in two parallel lines.

Say: Today's verse is from the book of Matthew. Matthew is one of the four Gospels and the Gospels tell us all about the life of Jesus. In this chapter, a few of Jesus's friends have gone to the tomb where he was buried, but when they arrived there, they got quite a surprise! They found the tomb was empty and an angel told them that Jesus had risen, just as he predicted. What exciting news! Today, we're going to practice this verse from Matthew to remind us that Jesus is stronger than death.

Step #2: Give the ball to a child at the end of one of the lines. Have them toss it to the first person in the line across from them, saying the first word of the verse as they do. The next child will toss ball to the next person in line (in the line across from them), saying the second word of the verse as they do. This process continues, tossing the ball back and forth down the lines, saying the verse along the way. If there are more words than kids, send the ball back up the line to the beginning child.

Wrap-up: Good work tossing the ball and saying the verse! I wonder if we could do it even faster this time? Let's try one more time, giving it a little extra speed along the way.

Bible Stories for This Activity

- Luke 24:23 They had even seen a vision of angels, who said that he was alive…
- Matthew 12:40 ….so the Son of Man will be in the heart of the earth three days

Activity 2

Resurrection Rolls

Step #1: Introduce the verse.

Step #2: Allow a child to read the verse or read it to the group yourself.

> **Say:** This verse is the ending of the Easter story. Can anyone tell me anything else about the Easter story? *(Allow answers).*

Step #3: Show kids a marshmallow.

> **Say:** Today, we're going to make a fun snack to remind us what happened on that first Easter. Let's imagine that this is the body of Jesus. We see that it is white and pure. Jesus was sinless. He died to pay for our sins. After he was dead, his friends took his body off the cross and laid it in a tomb. They put oil and spices on the body, as was the custom in those days. (Put melted butter on the marshmallow and sprinkle it with cinnamon and sugar.) After Jesus's body was prepared, he was wrapped in cloth and buried in a tomb.

Step #4: Pretend to bury Jesus's body *(the marshmallow)* by wrapping it in the crescent roll.

Step #5: Allow kids to repeat this process with their own. Place the rolls on a cookie sheet and put them in a 350 degree oven for 10 minutes.

> **Say:** After Jesus was buried, everyone waited. Can you imagine waiting three long days? What is something that you have had to wait a long time for? *(Allow answers)*

Step #6: After 10 minutes, remove the rolls from the oven. Carefully cut open one roll and show the group what is inside.

> **Say:** Wow! That's amazing. The "tomb" *(the roll)* is empty! Just like Jesus's tomb was empty on that first Easter morning. Go ahead and eat your snack. I am so glad that Jesus is alive!

Wrap-up: Can you imagine how surprised Jesus' friends and family were on Easter morning? They were expecting to go put more spices on Jesus and instead found the tomb empty! I am so glad that Jesus is more powerful than death.

Supplies:

- Access to an oven
- Crescent rolls
- Large marshmallows
- Butter, melted
- Cinnamon
- Sugar
- Cookie sheet

LEARNING STYLES	TYPE
TACTILE	FOOD

Bible Stories for Activities 2 and 3

- 1 Corinthians 15:3-5 Christ died for our sins… he was raised on the third day
- Romans 6:9 We know that Christ, death no longer has dominion over him
- Romans 5:10 While we were still enemies with God, Christ died for us
- John 3:16 God so loved the world…

Supplies:

- Watercolor paints and brushes
- Water
- Watercolor paper or white construction paper
- Black construction paper
- Scissors
- Glue
- Cross and semi-circle template on page 154

LEARNING STYLES	TYPE

TACTILE	CRAFT

Wrap-up: When we read the Bible, we learn right and wrong, and we learn how to make good decisions. Just like a candle or torch would help us find the path in the dark woods, God's Word helps us choose the right path in life.

Activity 3

The Cross at Sunset Picture

Step #1: Pass out watercolor paper or white construction paper along with watercolors and water. Instruct kids to paint a sunset across their entire paper. If kids are unsure how to paint a sunset, have them paint very wide lines of red, yellow, and orange on the page. After they are done painting, set the pictures aside to dry a bit.

Say: Today's verse comes from the book of Matthew. It is part of the Easter story, which is the heart of our Christian faith. Because we all have sin in our lives, we cannot go to God's perfect place, heaven. Unless someone else pays the penalty for our sins. That is exactly what Jesus did on the cross for us – he died to pay the price for our sins, so that we could live forever in heaven with God. It may seem like a sad story at first, but Jesus did not stay dead! Let's read our memory verse for today.

Step #2: Open your Bible and find Matthew 28:6. Allow a child to read the verse out loud or read it yourself to the group.

Say: In this verse, the angels are telling Jesus's friends the good news about his resurrection! Jesus did die on the cross for us, but he did not stay dead. What good news!

Step #3: Pass out the black construction paper and have children cut out a semi-circle *(to be Golgotha hill)* and a cross using the reproducible template on page 154. Children may choose to do one cross or three crosses.

Step #4: Glue the semi-circle hill to the bottom of the sunset page *(put glue on the black construction paper in case the watercolors are not yet dry)*. Add the crosses to the top of the hill.

At-Home Activity

Hello! Our verse today comes from the Easter account - it is the message from the angels to the women who visited his tomb early Easter morning. Even though Jesus told his friends and followers that he would rise on the third day, they were still pretty surprised!

Have you ever been surprised by something God has done? Maybe it is something that has happened in your own life, something you heard about, or maybe even something in the Bible itself. Spend some time this week talking about the surprising things that God has done.

He is not here; he has risen, just as he said. - Matthew 28:6a

Chapter 37 - Cross and Hill Template

Chapter 38

Be still, and know that I am God...
– Psalm 46:10

Theme:
God wants us to spend time with him.

Overview:
One of the most important things we can do is take the time to be still, pray, and listen to God.

Supplies:

- Poster of Psalm 46:10
- Watercolor paper or white construction paper
- Colored pencils
- Watercolor paints and brushes
- Lettering books (available at many libraries)
- Stickers
- Soft, quiet music to play in the background

LEARNING STYLES	TYPE	
TACTILE	CRAFT	VERSATILE

Activity 1

Bible Verse Art

Step #1: Make a sample project. Using lettering books *(or samples from online)*, write out the verse on a sheet of white paper with colored pencils. Use the watercolor paints to decorate the page or apply stickers as extra decorations.

Step #2: Introduce the verse.
  Say: Today our verse comes from the book of Psalms. I'll read the whole verse to you *(read verse from your Bible)*, but we're going to concentrate on just the beginning. Today, we're going to be still and create some works of art to remind us how great God is. I have some books here that will show you how to make fancy letters or you can use these letter stickers instead.

Step #3: Show kids your sample project.
  Say: This is a sample project that I made earlier. You can make something like this or something completely different. I'm going to play some quiet music as we work so we can practice being still and thinking about God.

Step #4: Allow kids time to work on their projects. When they are done, hang them up for display.

Wrap-up: These are some amazing works of art. God wants us to take time each day to think about him and to spend time with him. This was a good way to practice that habit.

Bible Stories for This Activity

- Psalm 100:3 Know that the Lord, he is God...
- Zechariah 2:13 Be silent before the Lord...

Activity 2

Quiet Game

Step #1: Introduce the verse
Say: Today, we're taking a closer look at Psalm 46:10. Would anyone like to read that verse out loud for us?

Step #2: Allow a child to read the verse or read it to the group yourself.
Say: In this verse, we are encouraged to be still and think about how great God is. It's not easy to be still, is it? It seems like from the moment we get out of bed in the morning, we have places to be and things to do. It can be hard to find a moment to spend time with God. Today, we're going to play a little game to see just how hard it is to be silent.

Step #3: Sit the kids in a circle facing each other
Say: Okay, in this game, we are all going to try and be still. You can move your faces, but you cannot move your bodies. And most importantly, you cannot make any noise. I'm going to keep track of the time and see how well we can do.

Step #4: Start the game and see if kids can be still for 10 seconds. If they succeed, congratulate them on being still and give them a chance to wiggle.

Step #5: Play another round, and increase the time to 30 seconds. If they succeed, congratulate them on being still and give them a chance to wiggle. If anyone in the group moves their body or talks, the round is over.

Step #6: Continue to play until kids can sustain 60 seconds of stillness (or until it is clear that they are not up for the task!)

Wrap-up: Wow. That was a pretty tough task. Why do you think it's so hard to be still in our lives? *(Allow answers).* Sometimes it seems like we have so many "important" things to do that we don't have time to be still and spend time with God, but being with God is actually the most important thing we could ever do. This week, I would encourage you to spend time when you wake up in the morning or when you are going to bed at time to be still and spend time with God.

Supplies:

• Stopwatch or clock

LEARNING STYLES	TYPE
AUDITORY	GAME

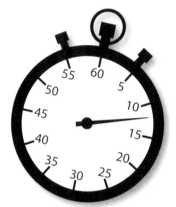

Bible Stories for Activities 2 and 3

• Psalm 62:1 My soul finds rest in God
• Psalm 1:1-2 Blessed in the man… who mediates on the law day and night
• Psalm 19:1 The heavens declare God's glory
• Psalm 100:3 Know that the Lord is God

Cloud Watching

Supplies:

- Warm day with fluffy clouds in the sky
- Blankets (optional)
- Reproducible page found on 158, one for each child
- Shoebox or other small box (one for each child)
- Scotch tape
- Scissors
- Yarn or twine

LEARNING STYLES		TYPE
VISUAL	TACTILE	CRAFT

Step #1: Introduce the verse.

Say: Today's verse comes from the book of Psalms. It was likely written by the sons of Korah. In this verse, we are told to be still and know that God is God. It is not always easy to be still, but today, we're going to give it a try.

Step #2: Lead the kids outside and have them lay on the blankets *(optional)* or on the grass.

Say: We're going to spend some time gazing at the sky and thinking about how great God is. We're going to be still except for our eyes. Let's look at the clouds and see if we can recognize any shapes.

Step #3: Allow kids to gaze at the sky and point out shapes or creatures they see in the sky.

Step #4: After a few minutes, take kids back inside and give them each a cloud page and scissors. Have them cut out the clouds and then tape them inside a small box, using the yarn to make it look like the clouds are floating in the air (tape yarn to the inside top of the box and to the back of the clouds).

Wrap-up: You guys did a great job with these projects. I hope that they will remind you to be still and think about God's greatness each day. Let's practice saying the verse a few more times as a group.

At-Home Activity

Hello! Today's verse comes from the book of Psalms. It is a verse that is certainly hard to put into practice in our busy culture. Our verse (read it below) tells us to be still and know that God is God. So often, it seems that our never-ending to-do list leaves little time to be still at all, let alone be still and think about God. It is in these moments of quiet and stillness that we often hear from the Lord. Do you have a regular time to spend with God each day? If so, how did you develop that habit? If not, what is keeping you from developing that habit? Talk with your children this week about the importance of spending time with God and come up with a plan so that each member of the family can have some stillness during the day to think about and be with God.

Be still, and know that I am God... - Psalm 46:10

Chapter 38 - Clouds

Chapter 39

Ask and it will be given to you; seek and you will find; knock and the door will be opened to you. – Matthew 7:7

Theme:
God wants to answer our prayers.

Overview:
When we seek God our priorities match what he wants to give us.

Supplies:

• Several small objects (button, paper clip, building brick man, tiny toys, earring, etc)

LEARNING STYLES	TYPE
LOGICAL	GAME

Activity 1

Ask and It Will Be Given Game

Step #1: Introduce the verse

Say: Today, our verse comes from the book of Matthew. It is something Jesus said while he was on earth. Would anyone like to read from their Bible?

Step #2: Allow a child to read the verse from a Bible or read it yourself to the kids.

Say: This is a pretty amazing promise we have from God. We can ask God for things when we pray to him. We're going to play a little game so you can practice asking for things.

Step #3: Secretly pick one of the small objects and hide it behind your back.

Say: We're going to go around the group and each person can ask a question about the object *(doesn't have to be a yes/ no question)*. When you think you have figured out what the object is, raise your hand and ask for it. If you ask correctly, the object will be given to you *(until we end the game)*.

Step #4: Allow kids to ask questions about the object until they are able to guess what it is. If they seem especially stumped, you can offer a few clues. At the end of each round, say the verse together as a group. Play again as time permits.

Wrap-up: Good guessing and asking! God loves to give good gifts to his children. Let's read about it more in Matthew. *(Read Matthew 7:7-11)*. I'm so glad that God loves us and that he loves to answer us when we pray to him.

Bible Stories for This Activity

• Matthew 21:22 Whatever you ask for in prayer, you shall receive, if you have faith
• John 14:13-14 Whatever you ask for... so that my Father may be glorified

Activity 2

Seek and You Will Find

Step #1: Introduce the verse

Say: In our verse today, Jesus tells his followers that when we seek, we will find. If we want to be closer to God or find him more in our lives, all we need to do is to seek after him. We can do that by reading the Bible, spending time in prayer, and attending church.

Step #2: Allow a child to read Matthew 7:7 from a Bible or read it to the group yourself.

Say: We're going to play a little game that will remind us to seek after God. Many of you have probably played it before – it is called hide and seek!

Step #3: Pick one child to count and have the rest of the kids hide as quickly as they can. Once the counter is done counting, they will head off in search of their friends. They should continue to search until they have found everyone else in the group or when they have given up. When all the children have been found, say the verse together as a group. Play again as time permits.

Wrap-up: It was fun to hide and to seek in this game, but thankfully God doesn't hide from us like this! God wants to be found by us and wants to have a relationship with us. Let's close by praying and thanking God for the opportunity to be close to him!

Supplies:

• Large area for kids to run and hide (possibly outside)

LEARNING STYLES	TYPE

KINESTHETIC	GAME

Bible Stories for Activities 2 and 3

• Deuteronomy 4:29 You will seek God... seek with all your heart
• Psalm 14:2 The Lord looks down from heaven for anyone who seeks God
• Psalm 145:18-19 The Lord is near to all who call on him in truth
• Luke 18:1-8 Parable of the Persistent Widow

Supplies:

- Table and chairs
- Reproducible matching sheet on page 162 (optional)
- Crayons or colored pencils

LEARNING STYLES	TYPE
AUDITORY	GAME

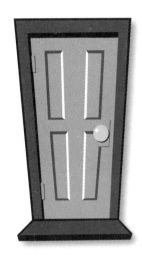

Knock Like Me

Step #1: Introduce the verse

Say: Today's verse comes from the book of Matthew. It has three promises in it. Go ahead and read it in your Bible and then let me know what the three promises are *(allow kids a chance to read and then answer the question).*

Step #2: Knock on the table

Say: We're going to play a little knocking game to help us remember the end of this verse. I'll knock out a simple rhythm on the table and then you will all try to copy me by knocking out the same rhythm.

Step #3: Knock on the table a simple short-long rhythm for the kids. Allow them to repeat the knock back to you. Increase the length of the knocking rhythm until it is clear that the kids can no longer keep up.

Step #4: If you have extra time, pass out copies of the door matching activity sheet for the kids to complete.

Wrap-up: That was some pretty fun knocking. Thankfully, we don't have to try that hard when we are trying to get God's attention. This part of the verse reminds us to be persistent in our prayer. To keep talking to God and "knocking on the door of heaven" until it is opened for us. Let's say the verse one more time as a group.

At-Home Activity

Hello! Today's verse comes from the book of Matthew. It is a verse that gives us instructions on how to pray and to seek after God. Of course, this verse doesn't mean that God will grant us our every wish – there are many other verses in the Bible that give us directions on what kinds of prayer God is looking for. This week, take a closer look at prayer with your family. Using a concordance or online search, find other verses in the Bible that have the word "prayer" in them. Make a chart or list that details the things you discovered about prayer and be sure to spend some time practicing prayer as well.

Ask and it will be given to you; seek and you will find;
knock and the door will be opened to you.
- Matthew 7:7

Chapter 39 - Door Matching Game

Knock and the door will be opened to you. **Matthew 7:7**

Look at the doors below and match the doors that are the same.

 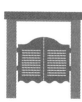    

Chapter 40

The Lord is my strength and my defense; he has become my salvation. He is my God, and I will praise him… – Exodus 15:2a

Theme:
God will help us.

Overview:
God is great and truly deserving of our praises.

Supplies:

- Strength and Song Activity sheet on page 166, one for each child
- Pencils or crayons
- Bibles

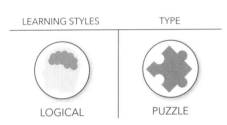

LEARNING STYLES	TYPE
LOGICAL	PUZZLE

Activity 1

Strength and My Song Matching Puzzle

Step #1: Pass out one of the activity sheets for each child (or you may want to let them work in pairs)

Say: In our verse today, a woman named Miriam and a man named Moses are praising God for what he has done. They explain that God has become their strength and their song. There are many other verses in the Bible that mention God's strength or a song that comes from God. Today, we're going to use our Bibles and do a little detective work.

Step #2: Pass out the Bibles

Say: You're going to look up the verse references on the left hand side and then match them to the correct verse on the right hand side.

Step #3: Allow children to work on their sheets. You may need to help them find certain verses if they are unfamiliar with the Bible.

Wrap-up: You guys did a great job finding these verses. Isn't it amazing how many times people praise God throughout the Bible? God is amazing and he is indeed our strength and song, just like he was for Miriam and Moses. Make sure you spend some time this week praising God for what he has done in your life.

Bible Stories for This Activity

- Psalm 75:1 We proclaim how great you are and tell of the wonderful things you have done.
- 1 Chronicles 16:28 Praise the Lord, all people on earth, praise his glory and might.

Note Card Scramble

Step #1: Prepare the note cards. Using markers, write one word of the verse on each note card. If you have a large group, you may want to prepare additional sets of cards, using the same method. Once the cards are complete, put each set inside a zippered plastic bag to keep them from getting mixed up with the other sets.

Step #2: Gather the group together.

Say: Today, we're learning a verse from the book of Exodus *(Read Exodus 15:2 to the kids).* In this verse, the Israelites have just been freed from slavery in Egypt. They were crossing the Red Sea in a miraculous way. God split the water for his people and then closed it back up again on Pharaoh and his army. God did some amazing things and the Israelites were happy to praise him.

Step #3: Show the kids one set of note cards.

Say: We're going to play a little word scramble with these note cards. I'll mix these cards up, hand them to you and then you'll need to put them back in order. I'll use this timer to see how fast you are and we'll keep track of the high score.

Step #4: Pass a set of note cards to the first volunteer and say the verse as a group before they begin. Keep track of their time and make a chart for the high score. If the other kids seem to be getting restless, use the additional sets of cards to turn the game into a race *(have 2-3 kids compete against each other instead of the clock)* instead. Be sure to read the verse out loud at the end of each race.

Wrap-up: Phew! That was some pretty crazy word scramble fun. After all that practice, do you think you can say the verse without any help? *(Allow volunteers to give it a try).* Nice job! Remember to keep practicing this week and praising God for all he has done.

Supplies:

- Note cards, one for each word of the verse
- Markers
- Additional set of cards (optional)
- Timer

LEARNING STYLES		TYPE
LOGICAL	KINESTHETIC	VERSATILE

Bible Stories for Activities 2 and 3

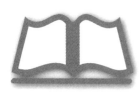

- Judges 5 Song of Deborah
- 2 Samuel 22 Song of David's deliverance
- Numbers 14:17 Now may the Lord's strength be displayed
- 2 Samuel 22:33 It is God who arms me with strength and keeps my way secure.

Praise God Posters

Supplies:

- White poster board, ½ sheet for each child
- Markers, crayons, or colored pencils
- Sticky tack to hang posters
- Bibles

LEARNING STYLES	TYPE

TACTILE	CRAFT

Step #1: Introduce the verse

> **Say:** Today our verse comes from the book of Exodus. This is a song that Moses and Miriam sang as the Israelite people were leaving Egypt and headed to the promise land. They are both proclaiming that the Lord is their strength and their song. He both protects them and makes their hearts happy. Let's take a quick look at the rest of the song to see why they are praising God.

Step #2: Read Exodus 15:1-19 from your Bible, encouraging kids to listen for specific things that Miriam and Moses are praising God for.

> **Say:** This passage talks about some amazing things that God did for his people, the Israelites, as they were escaping Egypt. Today, we're going to pretend that we were part of God's people back then. We're going to make a poster to record the great things that God did when he rescued his people from Egypt.

Step #3: Pass out the poster board and coloring utensils and allow kids time to work. Make Bibles available so kids can look at the passage again for ideas. Encourage kids to write the memory verse on the bottom of their poster.

Step #4: Once everyone is finished with their works of art, have them share them with the class, explaining what they chose to draw in their poster. Hang up posters with the sticky tack.

Wrap-up: You guys did an amazing job with these posters. God is great and truly deserving of our praises. Let's say our memory verse one more time before we finish.

At-Home Activity

Hello! Today, we started memorizing Exodus 15:2a (see verse below). The verse comes from a song written and sung by Moses and Miriam as they were exiting Egypt. Music is just as powerful today as it was in the Bible times. Do you have a favorite song that helps you praise God? Spend some time as a family sharing your favorite praise songs and listening to them together (great activity for the car!).

The Lord is my strength and my defense; he has become my salvation. He is my God, and I will praise him… - Exodus 15:2a

Chapter 40 - Strength and Song

Directions: Kids should use their Bible to look up the references on the right and match them with the verses on the left.

"Now may the Lord's strength be displayed, just as you have declared.	**Numbers 14:17**
It is God who arms me with strength and keeps my way secure.	**2 Samuel 22:33**
Look to the LORD and his strength; seek his face always.	**1 Chronicles 16:11**
Wealth and honor come from you; you are the ruler of all things. In your hands are strength and power to exalt and give strength to all.	**1 Chronicles 29:12**
They are your servants and your people, whom you redeemed by your great strength and your mighty hand.	**Nehemiah 1:10**
But you, LORD, do not be far from me. You are my strength; come quickly to help me.	**Psalm 22:19**
So Moses wrote down this song that day and taught it to the Israelites.	**Deuteronomy 31:22**
Hear this, you kings! Listen, you rulers! I, even I, will sing to the LORD; I will praise the LORD, the God of Israel, in song.	**Judges 5:3**
The LORD is my strength and my shield; my heart trusts in him, and he helps me. My heart leaps for joy, and with my song I praise him.	**Psalm 28:7**
You are my hiding place; you will protect me from trouble and surround me with songs of deliverance.	**Psalm 32:7**

Chapter 41

Blessed is the one whom God corrects; so do not despise the discipline of the Almighty. - Job 5:17

Overview:
God is our Heavenly Father. He makes sure we stay on the right path. Sometimes he has to correct us.

Supplies:
- Various medium sized objects (Frisbee, ball, helmet, doll, bucket, etc)
- Four chairs
- Yarn/rope
- Blindfold

LEARNING STYLES	TYPE
KINESTHETIC	GAME

Wrap-up: That was a pretty tough task! We can't always see the obstacles or dangers that we are getting close to, but God can. Sometimes he changes our course in order to keep us out of harm or to help us learn something. It might not make sense at the time, but God always wants what is best for us, and his discipline is to help us become more of the person he created us to be.

Activity 1

Course Correction

Step #1: Set up the playing area by tying up rope or yarn between chairs to show where the playing area is. Inside the playing area, place various medium objects on the ground, creating a maze.

Say: Today's verse comes from the book of Job. In this verse, Job's friend Eliphaz is speaking to him. Let's read it *(read Job 5:17)*. He reminds Job that God sometimes allows suffering and trials in our lives so that we will change something in our life or learn to depend more on God. It's kind of the same thing your parents do. When you do something wrong or dangerous, they correct you so that you will know better the next time. The discipline doesn't seem good at the time, but it helps us to become better people.

Step #2: Show kids the playing area.
Say: We're going to play a little game that is going to require some correction. I will select a volunteer to cross the playing field. The trick is, this volunteer will be blindfolded, so they are going to need some help. They can choose a partner who will give them directions as they cross the playing area.

Step #3: Select two volunteers. Blindfold one and instruct the other to watch where the blindfolded child is walking and give them clear directions and corrections in order to get across the playing area without touching anything. If the blindfolded child runs into anything or steps on anything, their turn is over.

Step #4: Continue to play, choosing two new volunteers for each round, as time allows.

Bible Stories for This Activity
- Psalm 94:12 Blessed is the man you discipline, O Lord.
- James 1:12 Blessed is the man who remains steadfast under trial

A Man Named Job

Step #1: Read Job 1 ahead of time, familiarizing yourself with the story.

Step #2: Make a copy of the clipart on page 170 and cut out each picture.

Step #3: Gather the children together and introduce the story.

Say: Today's verse comes from the book of Job. Job was a man who loved God and tried to keep his commandments. The Bible tells us that God had blessed Job and gave him great wealth and many things. There was a time in Job's life though, that God allowed Job to be tested. This was a hard time in Job's life.

Step #4: Read Job 1:1-3, Job 1:13-21 out loud to the kids *(or summarize in your own words)*. Display the pictures as they coordinate with the text (for example, show the picture of Job's children while reading verse 2). Display the pictures again when calamity befalls Job, but crumple them up when Job suffers loss *(for example, crumple up the picture of Job's children after reading verses 18-19)*.

Step #5: Summarize story and introduce the Memory Verse.

Say: This was terribly sad for Job, but Job still trusted the Lord through it all. We learn that sometimes God disciplines us to help us grow. It is sometimes hard, but our memory verse tells us that it is actually a blessing. Let's say the verse together *(Lead children in saying the memory verse)*.

Step #6: If there is extra time, have kids use their own copy of the clipart to create a picture or scene from the story *(optional)*. Encourage them to write the memory verse across the top or bottom of their page.

Wrap-up: Sometimes it seems like the Bible goes directly against what the world tells us. The world tells us that the "good life" is a worry free, trouble free life. But that's not what the Bible says. It says we are blessed when we go through hard times because it makes us a better person. It makes us more into the person that God wants us to be. It isn't always easy, but it is worth it. Let's say the verse one more time as a group!

Supplies:

- Copy and cut out page 170
- Additional clipart pages for the kids (optional)
- Construction paper, glue and crayons (optional)

LEARNING STYLES		TYPE
AUDITORY	VISUAL	STORY

Bible Stories for Activities 2 and 3

- 1 Peter 1:6-7 Rejoice in your trials… it shows the genuineness of your faith
- James 1:2 Consider it pure joy when you face trials of many kinds
- James 5:11 You have heard of the steadfastness of Job
- Romans 5:3-5 Our suffering produces perseverance…

Supplies:

- Dry erase board
- Dry erase markers and eraser

LEARNING STYLES		TYPE

 LOGICAL   GAME   VERSATILE

Activity 3

Guess that Letter

Step #1: Prepare the board. Write out the memory verse, using blanks for each of the individual letters. Write the alphabet across the top of the board and set up an area for keeping score *(boys vs. girls is always fun)*.

Say: Today, we're learning a verse from the book of Job. That's the only clue you're going to get though! It's your job to figure out what the verse is by guessing one letter at a time.

Step #2: Divide the kids into two teams.

Say: You will each get a chance to guess a letter. I'll erase the letters as we guess them, so you can keep track. Any time you guess a correct letter, you'll get 100 points for each time it is used *(similar to Wheel of Fortune)*.

Step #3: Select one player from the first team to guess a letter. Fill in the correct blanks if appropriate and erase the letter on the top. Award points if needed.

Step #4: Select one player from the second team and repeat the process. Continue taking turns between teams until all the letters are guessed or until someone can solve the puzzle.

Wrap-up: Way to go guys! You solved the puzzle and now we know our memory verse! Let's read it from the Bible *(read Job 5:17 from the Bible)*. To finish up, let's read it as a group from the board a few times.

At-Home Activity

Hello! Today, we started memorizing Job 5:17 (see verse below). The verse comes from the book of Job, which is full of heartache and hard times. In this book, we learn that our faith is often tested, but God is always with us. Have you ever had a hard time in your life where you felt like giving up on God? Have you had heartache that caused you to draw closer to God? Share one of these times with your kids this week. Pray together as a family that God will strengthen your faith and you will have his peace, no matter what life brings. Write the memory verse on a few note cards and put it near each family member's bed so they can read it before they go to sleep at night.

**Blessed is the one whom God corrects;
so do not despise the discipline of the Almighty.
- Job 5:17**

Chapter 41 – Job Story Images

Chapter 42

Blessed is the one....whose delight is in the law of the LORD, and who meditates on his law day and night. – Psalm 1:1-2

Theme:
God loves it when we read the Bible.

Overview:

God created the Bible so he can teach us the right ways to live. Our life is blessed when we follow it.

Supplies:

- Memory Verse Match Up sheet on page 174.
- Bibles

LEARNING STYLES	TYPE
KINESTHETIC	GAME

Activity 1

Memory Verse Review Game

Step #1: Make several copies of the memory verse match up page (one sheet for each team).

Step #2: Divide your groups into teams of 2 and give each team a memory verse page. Have them briefly look over the sheet and then cut along the dotted lines, separating the verses.

Say: In this game, you will have to match the beginning of the verse with the end of the verse. You are welcome to look in your Bibles for help, and the fastest team to pair up all the verses wins. There might be some verses that we've learned together or perhaps verses you've learned with your family. Memorizing Bible verses is a great way to delight in the law of the Lord (*which is our verse for today!*).

Step #3: Make sure kids mix up all the memory verse cards and stack them in a pile on the table. When you say "go", kids will compete to complete the pairs as quick as they can. Make Bibles available in case they need to look something up.

Step #4: After all the kids have completed the pairings, declare a winner and play again as time permits.

Wrap-up: You might have been surprised at how many of those verses you could easily pair up. That's the wonderful thing about Scripture – the more we memorize, the more God can bring just the right verse to our mind when we need it. Keep on practicing and reading the Bible so that it can help you in whatever situation you're in.

Bible Stories for This Activity

- Matthew 4:4 Man does not live on bread alone, but on every word…
- Colossians 3:16 Let the message of Christ dwell among you richly as you teach…

Books of the Bible Hopscotch Game

Step #1: Set up the hopscotch game by either drawing a hopscotch board on the butcher paper or by laying out the construction paper in a hopscotch pattern. Write the names of the Old Testament (or the New Testament) books of the Bible on the spaces *(one book per space)*. Tape the paper into place with the painter's tape or masking tape.

Step #2: Show kids the playing area and have them take off their shoes.

Say: Today's verses come from the book of Psalms. I'll read the complete passage to you, but we're only going to concentrate on a small part *(read Psalm 1:1-2)*. This verse tells us blessed is the man who delights in the law of the Lord – the Bible. One of the ways that we can delight in the Bible is by learning where all the books of the Bible are. This way, when we need to look up a certain verse, we will know right where to go.

Step #3: Line up the kids behind the hopscotch game.

Say: You will each have a turn to jump through the hopscotch game. As your feet touch each book of the Bible, say it out loud. I will time you to see who can get through the board the quickest. Remember though, you have to say all the books correctly for it to count. I'll give it a try first so you can see what to do and hear all the names of the books.

Step #4: Go through the hopscotch board yourself, saying the books of the Bible loudly and clearly for all to hear.

Step #5: Allow each child to give it a try, timing them as they go.

Wrap-up: There are a lot of books in the Bible. We might not be able to learn them all today, but with some practice, you can certainly do it! Let's say the memory verse together as a group to finish off our time together.

Supplies:

- Very long roll of paper or
- Package of construction paper
- Painters tape or masking tape
- Marker
- Timer

LEARNING STYLES	TYPE
KINESTHETIC	GAME

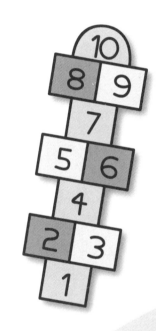

Bible Stories for Activities 2 and 3

- Joshua 1:8 You should meditate on it day and night
- Psalm 119:11 I have hidden your word in my heart
- 1 Thessalonians 3:10 Night and day we pray most earnestly....
- Psalm 42:8 By day the LORD directs his love, at night his song is with me

Supplies:

- Large area to run around in

LEARNING STYLES	TYPE

KINESTHETIC	GAME

Activity 3

Day and Night Tag

Step #1: Gather the kids together. Select one person to be "it".

Say: Today, we're learning a verse from the book of Psalms. In this verse, we learn that we are blessed (that's a good thing!) when we delight in the law of the Lord. When we delight in the law of the Lord, this means that we enjoy reading the Bible and learning more about God. The verse encourages us to meditate (think about) on the Bible both day and night. In this game, we're going to play a different version of freeze tag. You will begin by playing freeze tag normally, but when I say a few key words, you will change the way you move.

Step #2: Introduce the key words

Say: The key words in this verse are "delight", "day", and "night". I will say the verse out loud randomly throughout the game, emphasizing one of these key words. Whenever you hear one of these key words very loudly, you'll change the way you move. Here's how:

Delight: Start hopping around excitedly
Day: Walk or run like normal
Night: Crawl on the ground like you're exhausted

Step #3: Start the game, changing the key word about every 30 seconds *(be sure to say the whole verse, emphasizing just one word)*. When everyone is frozen or when about 3 minutes have passed, have everyone stop and choose a new "it". Play again as time permits.

Wrap-up: That was a fun way to learn our memory verse. Does anyone think they can say it on their own? *(Allow children to give it a try)*. Let's all say it together to finish up.

At-Home Activity

Hello! Today, we started memorizing Psalm 1:1-2 (see verse below). This passage tells us that we will be blessed when we meditate on (think about) the Bible both day and night. Do you have a time when you regularly read God's Word or think about it? Do your children? How can you begin a routine in your home that includes delighting in the law of the Lord? This week, take a few minutes before bed at night to read a short portion of Scripture together. Talk with each other at the end of the week about the difference it made in your life.

**Blessed is the one….whose delight is in the law of the LORD,
and who meditates on his law day and night.**
- Psalm 1:1-2

Chapter 42 - Memory Verse Match Up

Act justly, love mercy	And walk humbly with your God. Micah 6:8
Give thanks to the Lord, for he is good.	His love endures forever. Psalm 136:1
Your word is a lamp to my feet	and a light for my path. Psalm 119:105
Trust in the LORD with all your heart	and lean not on your own understanding. Proverbs 3:5
I can do all things through	Christ who strengthens me. Philippians 4:13
Blessed is the one whose delight is in the law of the LORD,	and who meditates on his law day and night. Psalm 1:1-2

Chapter 43

In your anger do not sin: Do not let the sun go down while you are still angry.
– Ephesians 4:26

Theme:
God wants us to control our anger.

Overview:
Sometimes it is okay to be angry. God wants us to ask him for help so we don't take our anger too far.

Supplies:
• Poster of Ephesians 4:26

LEARNING STYLES	TYPE
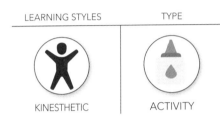	
KINESTHETIC	ACTIVITY

Activity 1

Getting the Anger Out

Step #1: Gather kids together and introduce the verse.

Say: Today, we're learning a verse about anger. Do you ever get angry about anything? *(Allow kids to answer).* Sure - we all get angry about stuff once in awhile. The Bible tells us that it's okay to get angry - but we cannot sin because of this anger. What are some sins that might happen when we are angry? *(Allow answers).* That's right - we might hit someone, say something unkind, or even purposely leave someone out when we are angry. These things are wrong. Today, we're going to learn some other ways to deal with our anger.

Step #2: Have kids stand up.

Say: Does anyone have a tactic they use to get the anger out without sinning? Have kids share answers and if applicable, have the rest of the group practice the tactics. If you need extra suggestions, try some of these:
- Pray and ask God for help.
- Counting slowly to 10
- Breathing in and out slowly
- Angry face
- Pretend to blow out 10 candles
- Press palms of hands together hard for 10 seconds
- Give yourself a time out
  (go somewhere where you can be calm)

Wrap-up: It's not always easy to control our anger, but it will get easier the more you practice. God will give us the strength to do things that we cannot do on our own, if we only ask him. Let's pray and ask God to keep us from sinning when we get angry this week. After that, we'll say the verse a few times as a group.

Bible Stories for This Activity

- Proverbs 29:11 A fool gives full vent to his anger, but a wise man keeps himself under control.
- Genesis 4:2-8 Cain and Abel

Activity 2

Let It Go

Step #1: Gather the kids together and introduce the verse.

Say: Today we're learning a verse from Ephesians. Would anyone like to read this verse from their Bible? *(Allow a volunteer to read or read from the Bible yourself)*. It's normal *(and okay!)* to get angry sometimes, but the Bible tells us that we should not sin when we are angry and we should not hang on to that anger *(letting the sun go down)*.

Step #2: Show kids the balloon.

Say: We're going to imagine that this is a person. This person is getting mad *(blow a little air into the balloon)*, and instead of trying to let the anger go… he keeps thinking about it *(blow into the balloon)* and thinking about it *(blow into the balloon)* and thinking about it *(blow into the balloon)*. He could have tried to calm down or even prayed and asked God for help, but he didn't. He said some mean words *(blow into the balloon)* and just kept thinking about how mad he was *(blow into the balloon)*. What do you think will happen if he keeps dwelling on his anger? *(Allow answers)*. Yes – he will probably explode. He might hit someone, push them, or sin in some other way. This is not what God wants for our lives. He wants us to let our anger go *(let go of the balloon, letting it fly all over the room if you want)*.

Wrap-up: It's not always easy to let go of our anger. Sometimes we need to talk with a parent or friend so we can work through something, but God makes it very clear that he doesn't want us to hurt others when we are angry. This week, whenever you get angry – I want you to remember this balloon and practice letting the anger go before it leads you into sin.

Supplies:

- Balloon (you may want extras for the kids to take home)

LEARNING STYLES	TYPE
VISUAL	OBJECT LESSON

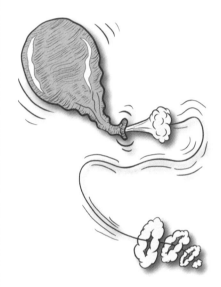

Bible Stories for Activities 2 and 3

- James 1:19-20 Be quick to listen and slow to anger
- 1 Samuel 25 David and Nabel (David almost sinned in his anger)
- Ecclesiastes 7:9 Be not quick in your spirit to become angry…
- Proverbs 14:29 Whoever is slow to angry has great understanding…

Supplies:

- Red paint, yellow paint, orange paint
- Sturdy paper
- Paint brushes and rinsing water
- Small cups to put the paint into
- Smocks
- Permanent markers
- Poster of Ephesians 4:26
- Wet wipes

LEARNING STYLES	TYPE
 TACTILE	CRAFT

Sunset Art

Step #1: Set up the supplies before the kids arrive – making small stations where 3-4 kids can work together. When the kids arrive, make sure everyone puts on a smock.

Say: Today, we're learning a verse from the book of Ephesians. Ephesians was written by a man named Paul to the church in Ephesus. This book gives us instructions on how to live as followers of Christ *(Christians)*. I'll read the verse we're learning about today *(read Ephesians 4:26 from your Bible)*. In this verse, we are commanded to not let the sun go down on our anger. It is okay to be angry once in awhile, but we should not hold onto that anger. We should try to fix the problem and make things right with whoever we are angry with before the day is done.

Step #2: Pass out the paper.

Say: We are going to create a picture of a sunset today to remind us of our memory verse. Before you begin to paint your sunset, I want you to write Ephesians 4:26 on the top or bottom of your page.

Step #3: Allow kids time to work on their projects, setting them aside to dry when they are finished.

Wrap-up: Nice work on these art projects. Let's finish up by practicing the verse a few more times as a group.

**Send home a set of "How do you feel" cards – page 178.
Try to copy onto cardstock for extra durability.**

At-Home Activity

Hello! Today we learned a verse from the New Testament book of Ephesians. We all get angry at times, and that's okay. The important thing is to not sin because of our anger. It's amazing all the different emotions we can experience – sometimes even on the same day! Use the cards you got at church to play a game of "How Do You Feel" go fish. Deal out 4 cards to each player. Take turns asking each other for a match. The person who has the most matches at the end of the game wins. After each round, say the memory verse together as a family (found below).

**In your anger do not sin:
Do not let the sun go down while you are still angry.
- Ephesians 4:26**

How Do I Feel Cards

Chapter 44

A gentle answer turns away wrath, but a harsh word stirs up anger.
– Proverbs 15:1

Theme:
God wants us to control our anger.

Overview:
The Holy Spirit can help you give people kindness even if they are mean to you.

Supplies:
- Cotton balls
- Sand paper

LEARNING STYLES	TYPE
TACTILE	OBJECT LESSON

Optional:
If you have extra time, you could bring extra sandpaper and cotton balls to have the kids create an art project that focuses on the memory verse.

Activity 1

Sandpaper and Cotton Balls

Step #1: Gather kids together and introduce the verse.
Say: Today, we're learning a verse about our words. The verse is found in the book of Proverbs. Let's read it together. *(You or a volunteer read Proverbs 15:1)*

Step #2: Show the kids the cottons balls *(or some other soft object)*. Walk around the room and let the children feel it *(or rub it on their arm so they can feel it)*.
Say: In our verse, we read that a gentle (or soft) answer will turn away wrath. This means that when we speak kindly or gently to others, they will not get angry with us. What are some soft or gentle things you might say to someone? *(Allow answers)*. What happens if someone is already mad at you? What gentle answer might you say to turn away their anger? *(Allow answers)*

Step #3: Show the kids the sandpaper. Walk around the room and allow children to feel the rough part of the sandpaper with their fingers.
Say: On the other hand, our verse also tells us that harsh (or rough) words will stir up anger. This sandpaper reminds me of harsh or rough words that we could say. It doesn't feel good to touch. What are some harsh things that we might say to one another? What are some harsh things someone might have said to you? *(Allow answers)*.

Wrap-up: Sometimes it's hard to respond in kindness when people are being mean to us. If someone speaks to us in anger, it's easy to yell right back. But that's not the way God wants us to live. It's not always easy, but the Holy Spirit gives us strength to give gentle answers when faced with someone else's anger. Let's pray and ask God for strength to give gentle answers instead of harsh words this week.

Bible Stories for This Activity
- 1 Peter 3:9 Do not repay evil with evil or insult with insult.
- Romans 12:17 Do not repay anyone evil for evil.

Activity 2

T-shirt Memory Verse Scramble

Step #1: Prepare the shirts.

Say: On the blank side of each T-shirt, write one word of the memory verse with the permanent marker. Be sure to include the reference on one shirt as well. Set shirts aside for now.

Step #2: Introduce the verse

Say: Today we're learning a verse from the book of Proverbs. Does anyone know who wrote the book of Proverbs? *(Allow answers).* Solomon wrote the book of Proverbs and it is full of wisdom for how we should live our lives. Let's read our memory verse from the Bible *(You or a volunteer read Proverbs 15:1).* This verse tells us that a gentle answer will help make a situation better – it will help get rid of any anger. On the other hand, a harsh answer will just stir up more problems. Today, we're going to learn the verse in a creative way.

Step #3: Pass out the shirts to the kids. If you have more kids than shirts, some will serve as the audience *(they will read the verse at the end).* If this is the case, plan on playing a few rounds so everyone gets a chance to wear a shirt. Help kids put a shirt on over their regular clothing so the words you wrote are facing the front. If you have more shirts than kids, you could arrange a few shirts on a make-shift clothesline and have the kids fill in the blanks.

Step #4: When you say "go" kids should arrange themselves in order so they spell out the verse correctly. When everyone is in the proper place, have the audience read the verse out loud. This would also be a great time to take a picture! Play again as time permits, mixing up the shirts so everyone gets a different word each time.

Wrap-up: That was a pretty mixed up way to practice our verse! Does anyone think they can say it on their own (allow kids to try). Nice job everyone. Remember to practice saying kind words this week.

Supplies:

- 14 T-shirts with a blank front or blank back
- Permanent marker for writing on shirts

LEARNING STYLES	TYPE	
KINESTHETIC	GAME	VERSATILE

Tip:
Grab some cheap t-shirts at a local thrift store or ask friends and families to donate a few.

Bible Stories for Activities 2 and 3

- James 1:19-20 Be quick to listen and slow to anger
- 1 Kings 12 Israel rebels against Rehoboam because of his harsh words
- Proverbs 25:15 With patience, a ruler may be persuaded
- Proverbs 28:25 A greedy man stirs up strife

Supplies:

- Two cans of carbonated soda
- Outdoor space

LEARNING STYLES	TYPE
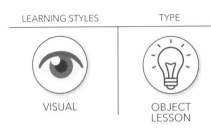	
VISUAL	OBJECT LESSON

Bonus Activity:
Copy Verse Cards on page 182. Use this game to fill in extra time.

Shaking Up Anger

Step #1: Gather children and head outside. Have them sit on the grass or pavement (a few feet away from you).

Say: Today, we're learning a verse from the book of Proverbs. Proverbs was written by a king named Solomon. Solomon was the wisest man who ever lived and the book of Proverbs is full of his wisdom. Let me read the verse for you *(read Proverbs 15:1)*.

Step #2: Show the kids one can of soda.

Say: Have you ever been in a situation where people started getting mad or irritated with each other? It seems like one person says something harsh *(shake can)* and then the other person does the same thing *(shake can)* and before you know it, someone is ready to explode! *(Open up the can of soda and let it spray into the air)*

Step #3: Show the kids the other can of soda.

Say: On the other hand, Proverbs 15:1 tells us that a gentle answer turns away wrath, or anger *(set the can down gently and then open it slowly)*.

Wrap-up: It sure is hard to give a gentle answer when someone is being harsh with us, isn't it? Sometimes we need to walk away, or count to 10 - or something like that before we can give a gentle answer. Often, we can't do it on our own - we need to pray and ask for help from the Holy Spirit. The more we practice gentleness in the face of anger, the easier it will get. Let's say the verse together as a group before we head off.

At-Home Activity

Hello! Today, we began to learn Proverbs 15:1 as a group (see verse below). Have you recently been a situation when someone was speaking harshly to you? Did you give a gentle answer in return? Why or why not?

Share this incident with your children and brainstorm ways that you can all give a gentle answer when a situation like this arises again. Pray together that God will give you strength to turn away from anger and do the right thing instead.

**A gentle answer turns away wrath,
but a harsh word stirs up anger.
- Proverbs 15:1**

Chapter 44 - Memory Verse Fun

Here are some fun ways to say the memory verse. Have each child select a card (put on the table face down) and then go around the room, having each child say the verse in the way their card describes.

Plug your nose and say the verse	Stand on one leg and say the verse
Do a somersault as you say the verse	Say the verse with your eyes closed
Say the verse while tapping your head	Say the verse while jogging in place
Say the verse while pretending to look in a mirror	Say the verse while pretending to type on a computer
Say the verse in a little bird voice	Say the verse in a big bear voice
Say the verse ultra slow	Say the verse ultra fast

Chapter 45

In the morning, LORD, you hear my voice; in the morning I lay my requests before you and wait expectantly. – Psalm 5:3

Theme:
We can bring our requests to God.

Overview:
God loves us and wants us to talk to him. He loves to give good gifts to his children.

Supplies:
- Bean bag or other small object to serve as "the bacon"
- Large playing area
- Washable markers (optional)

LEARNING STYLES

KINESTHETIC

TYPE

GAME

Activity 1

Waiting Expectantly Game (Steal the Bacon)

Step #1: Divide your group up into two even teams. Give each person a number (you may want to write the number on each child's hand with washable marker if the kids are prone to forgetting). The numbers should be the same for each team (for example, if Team A has a child with the #1, Team B should also have a child with the #1).

Say: We're going to play a little game called steal the bacon. You are going to wait *expectantly* for your number to be called. When I call a number, whoever has that number on Team A will run out and also whoever has that number on Team B will run out. You will both try to grab this "bacon". The object of the game is to grab the bacon and get back to your team without getting tagged. You get one point if you can successfully get the bacon back to your team. You can also get a point if you tag your opponent once they have grabbed the "bacon".

Step #2: Line kids up on opposite walls and put the "bacon" in the middle of the room. Call a number and encourage the two opposing kids to grab the "bacon". Award points as needed. Play until all kids have had a chance to play.

Wrap-up: This game reminds me a lot of a verse in the book of Psalms. Let's read it from the Bible (read Psalm 5:3). In this verse, David says that he prays in the morning and then waits expectantly for God to answer. Just like you were waiting expectantly for your number to be called, that's how David waited for God. God loves to hear us pray and we know that he loves to give good gifts to his children.

Bible Stories for This Activity
- Matthew 7:11   God loves to give good gifts to his children
- Ephesians 6:18   Be alert and persistent in your prayers…

Activity 2

Do You Hear My Voice?

Step #1: Gather kids together and introduce the verse.

Say: Today, we're learning a verse about praying. The verse is found in the book of Psalms. Let's read it together *(You or a volunteer read Psalm 5:3)*

Step #2: Have the kids sit in a circle on the floor.

Say: In our verse, we read that we can bring our requests to the Lord and he hears our voice. What an amazing thing! God can hear all of the things we prayer, no matter when we pray or where we pray. He can even hear more than one person at the same time! In this game, we're going to see how well you do at hearing. I'm going to whisper something to a friend and they will have to pass it on to the next person until it makes it all the way around the circle.

Step #3: Sit in the circle with the kids and whisper a wacky sentence to the person sitting next to you. Kids should continue to whisper to each other all around the circle (this is the "telephone" game) until it gets to the last person. That person will say the sentence out loud and you'll reveal what the original sentence was. Play again as time permits. Here are some sentences to get you started:

- Noisy Nelly needs some nuggets for her new house.
- Carrie the cat sits on a hat eating her curds and whey.
- Brown bunnies bust into a barn, banging on a banjo as they go.
- The red rooster rustled up some grub, grabbing some red roses along the way.
- Ted the turtle had a burger and then began to cry.

Wrap-up: That was a pretty funny game! I'm so glad that God doesn't get our requests all mixed up like that! God hears what we are saying all the time, even when we only say the request in our heart. God loves it when we pray to him, morning or night.

Supplies:

- None

LEARNING STYLES	TYPE

AUDITORY	GAME

Tip:
To add some fun and magnify the sound, use a paper towel tube to whisper to each other

Bible Stories for Activities 2 and 3

- 1 John 5:14 If we ask anything according to his will, he hears us.
- Psalm 17:6 …turn your ear to me and hear my prayer.
- Joshua 10 The sun stands still
- Genesis 1 The creation of the sun

Supplies:

- Yellow construction paper
- Blue construction paper
- Glue
- Scissors (optional)
- Sample project

LEARNING STYLES	TYPE

TACTILE | CRAFT

Attach letter on page 186
to At-Home Activity

Attach letter on page 186
to At-Home Activity

Activity 3

In the Morning (Art Project)

Step #1: Introduce the verse.

Say: Today, we're learning a verse from the book of Psalms. Much of the book of Psalms was written by a man named David. David was a man who loved God, and you can see this in many of the poems and songs that he wrote. In this verse, David is praying to God in the morning and then waiting for God to answer. Let's read the verse together.

Step #2: Read Psalm 5:3 from your Bible or have a volunteer read it to the group.

Say: Do you spend time in the morning praying? Some people love to get up with the sun and spend a few minutes with God, talking to him and laying their requests before him. For this craft, we're going to make a sun out of tiny pieces of paper so that it will look like a mosaic.

Step #3: Show the kids your sample artwork and demonstrate how to cut or tear the construction paper up into tiny pieces to create a mosaic. Give each child one yellow piece and one blue piece of paper and allow them to begin tearing (or cutting).

Step #4: When kids have completed tearing the paper, give them a second piece of blue construction paper and have them glue the tiny pieces onto it in the shape of a sun. You may wish to play some quiet praise music in the background as they work.

Wrap-up: These are some really unique suns! I love all the little details on those small pieces of paper. Do you know that God hears every single detail of our prayers? He hears the short prayers and the long prayers and he cares about all of them. I hope when you see your sun art project this week, you will remember to bring your requests to the Lord.

At-Home Activity

Hello! Today, we began to learn Psalm 5:3 as a group (see verse below). There are lots of verses in Psalms and Proverbs that work well as memory verses. Use the attached paper to play a little game of memory verse memory!

Step #1: Cut cards apart on the black lines
Step #2: Lay cards face down on the table
Step #3 Take turns flipping over the cards. If you get a match, you get to keep the cards.
Step #4: Whoever has the most matches at the end of the game, wins.

In the morning, LORD, you hear my voice; in the morning I lay my requests before you and wait expectantly. - Psalm 5:3

Chapter 45 - Psalms and Proverbs

Your word is a lamp to my feet and a light for my path. (Psalm 119:105)

Your word is a lamp to my feet and a light for my path. (Psalm 119:105)

Trust in the LORD with all your heart and lean not on your own understanding. (Proverbs 3:5)

Trust in the LORD with all your heart and lean not on your own understanding. (Proverbs 3:5)

The heavens declare the glory of God; the skies proclaim the work of his hands." Psalm 19:1

The heavens declare the glory of God; the skies proclaim the work of his hands." Psalm 19:1

God is our refuge and strength, a very present help in trouble. (Psalm 46:1)

God is our refuge and strength, a very present help in trouble. (Psalm 46:1)

Oh give thanks to the LORD, for He is good, for His loving kindness is everlasting." (Psalm 107:1)

He who walks with wise men will be wise, but the companion of fools will suffer harm." (Proverbs 13:20)

Delight yourself in the Lord and he will give you the desires of your heart. Commit your way to the Lord, trust in him and he will do this. (Psalm 37:4-5)

I have hidden your word in my heart that I might not sin against you. (Psalm 119:11)

Let everything that has breath praise the LORD. Praise the LORD. (Psalm 150:6)

Give thanks to the Lord, for he is good. His love endures forever. (Psalm 136:1)

Be still, and know that I am God. (Psalm 46:10)

Blessed is the man ... whose delight is sin the law of the Lord (Psalm 1:2)

Chapter 46

I will sing the LORD's praise,
for he has been good to me.
– Psalm 13:6

Theme:
Singing is a way to praise the Lord.

Overview:
No matter how well you sing, God loves to hear our praises to him.

Supplies:

• Poster of the memory verse

LEARNING STYLES		TYPE

AUDITORY	MUSIC	ACTIVITY

Activity 1

Guest Musician

Step #1: Invite a friend, family member, or church member who has musical talent to be a guest for your group. Ask them to prepare a short song to sing for the kids. Encourage them to share their story with the kids (*how did they get started, what kind of songs do they like to sing, etc*).

Step #2: Introduce the verse and guest musician.

Say: Today, we're learning a verse from the book of Psalms. Many of the Psalms are actually songs. In this particular Psalm, the author is saying how he likes to praise God through singing. Let's read the verse from the poster together.

Step #3: Lead the kids in reading the verse from your poster.

Say: We've got a special treat today. We have a guest who is going to praise the Lord through singing. Let's listen in and then afterwards, you can ask questions.

Step #4: Encourage kids to sit quietly and listen to the music and then to ask questions afterwards.

Wrap-up: Let's say thank you to our special guest today. He/she certainly praised the Lord through singing. Let's say the verse all together a few more times to help us remember that we can praise the Lord through singing anytime.

Bible Stories for This Activity

• Ezra 3:11 They sang, praising and giving thanks to the LORD
• Psalm 147:7 Sing to the LORD with thanksgiving; Sing praises to our God on the lyre…

Sing to the Lord

Step #1: Pick out 2-3 popular worship songs that you think your kids will especially like. Print off the lyrics for the songs *(or maybe just the chorus if the songs are especially long)*. Gather kids together in a group.

Say: Our verse today is all about praising the Lord through singing. Would anyone like to read the verse? *(You or a volunteer to read Psalm 13:6).* Singing is a great way to praise the Lord. Let's take a closer look at some popular praise songs.

Step #2: Pass the song lyrics to the kids and have them read over them. Discuss the songs as a group. Here are some questions to get you started:
- Where do you think the inspiration for this song came from?
- Does any part of this song remind you of Scripture?
- What is your favorite part of the song?
- What kind of emotions do you think of when you read the words of this song?

Step #3: After taking a look at the lyrics, play the songs for the kids, encouraging them to sing along with the words.

Wrap-up: You guys were great at singing these songs. What are some other ways we can praise the Lord? The great thing about singing is that it can be done almost anywhere! You don't have to be in church to praise the Lord through song. You can do it in your bedroom, in the car, or even in the shower! Keep on praising the Lord.

Supplies:

- CDs of popular worship songs or DVD kids can sing along with
- CD play or DVD player and TV
- Computer, internet access (to look up lyrics), and printer

LEARNING STYLES	TYPE
AUDITORY	ACTIVITY

Another option:
If your kids aren't comfortable singing together as a group, you might want to bring in some pillows instead and have them lay down or relax while listening to a few songs as a group.

Bible Stories for Activities 2 and 3
- Psalm 21:13 Be exalted, Oh Lord… We will sing and praise your power.
- Psalm 96:1 Sing to the Lord a new song
- 2 Samuel 22 David sings a praise song to the Lord
- Colossians 3:16 ….singing songs and hymns…

Praise Him Alphabet

Supplies:

- Praise the Lord reproducible sheet on page 190.
- Pencils or pens
- Praise music and CD player (to play music in the background, optional)

LEARNING STYLES	TYPE
LOGICAL	PUZZLE

Step #1: Introduce the verse.

Say: Today, we're learning a verse from the book of Psalms. This Psalm was written by David, like many of the Psalms. In this verse, David is saying that he will praise God through singing. Let's read the verse together.

Step #2: Read Psalm 13:6 from your Bible or have a volunteer read it to the group.

Say: Do you ever sing praises to the Lord? What are some of your favorite songs to sing? If you were going to write a song, what kind of things would you praise God for? *(Allow answers)*

Step #3: Pass out one of the "Praise the Lord" Alphabet pages to each child. Make pens or pencils available.

Say: We're going to play a little game as we praise the Lord. Let's try to think of things to praise God for, using each letter of the alphabet *(you may want to let them use "X" in any part of the word!)*.

Step #4: Allow kids time to work, playing praise music in the background.

Wrap-up: Let's hear some of the things that you can praise God for *(bonus if you sing your list!)*. God is amazing and he blesses us in so many ways.

*** Would work with any verse ***

At-Home Activity

Hello! Today, we began to learn Psalm 13:6 as a group (see verse below). You are encouraged to continue learning this verse as a family during the week. Here's a few fun games to play to help you learn the verse together:

Toss Across: Toss a ball to one family member. Have him say the first word of the verse before tossing the ball to someone else, who then says the next word, and so on. Continue until you complete the verse. If the ball is dropped, start over again. Time how long it takes to finish the verse; and try to beat the previous time.

Clap the Missing Word: Write the verse on a note card and give it to one family member. Have them read the verse out loud, skipping one word and clapping instead. Have the other family members try to guess the word that was "clapped" out.

I will sing the LORD's praise, for he has been good to me. - Psalm 13:6

Chapter 46 - Praise the Lord

Can you think of something to praise the Lord for that starts with every letter of the alphabet?

A _____

B _____

C _____

D _____

E _____

F _____

G _____

H _____

I _____

J _____

K _____

L _____

M _____

N _____

O _____

P _____

Q _____

R _____

S _____

T _____

U _____

V _____

W _____

X _____

Y _____

Z _____

Chapter 47

When I am afraid, I put my trust in you.
- Psalm 56:3

Theme:
God will be with us when we are afraid.

Overview:
God is bigger than all our worries. We can trust him when we are afraid.

Supplies:
- Blindfold (optional)
- Pillows (optional)
- At least 7 kids (3 on each side of the line, and one volunteer to fall)

LEARNING STYLES	TYPE
KINESTHETIC	ACTIVITY

Activity 1

Trust Fall

Step #1: Introduce the verse.

Say: Today, we are learning a verse from the book of Psalms. It tells us that when we are afraid, we can trust in God. Sometimes it's scary to trust in God - to wait and see if he is going to fix the problem or provide for our needs. However, we must remember that God loves us and wants what is best for us. We can trust him when we are afraid.

Step #2: Select a volunteer to try the trust fall first. You may wish to blindfold them.

Say: We're going to practice trusting each other today. Let's line up in two lines, equal amounts of kids on either side. Put your arms out straight, palms up. *(You may wish to lay down pillows in between the two lines, where the volunteer will fall - just in case!)* Our volunteer is going to say the memory verse and then fall backwards. Your job is to catch them.

Step #3: Have the volunteer cross their hands across their chest and close their eyes. After they say the memory verse, they should fall straight back without bending their knees.

Step #4: Make sure kids are taking their task seriously and showing that they are trust worthy. Let a few kids try falling as time permits.

Wrap-up: I bet it wasn't easy to fall backwards like that, not knowing exactly when you would be caught. Sometimes life is like that too - we know that we can trust God, but we don't exactly know when (or how!) he will intervene. However, the Bible tells us that God will be with us, and when we are afraid, we can trust in him.

Bible Stories for This Activity
- Joshua 1:9 Be strong and courageous. Do not be afraid; do not be discouraged...
- Psalm 9:10 Those who know your name trust in you...

Activity 2

Ping Pong Balls and Egg Cartons (Race)

Step #1: Prepare the ping pong balls. Using the permanent marker, write one word of the verse on each of the ping pong balls. Don't forget to write the reference on one ball. Make one set for each team *(kids will be divided into teams of 5-6)*. Put each set into a bucket or bowl.

Say: Today, we're learning a verse from the book of Psalms. It's a pretty short verse and I bet you will have it learned by the time we are done! We're going to play a game to help us learn the verse.

Step #2: Divide the kids up into teams of 5-6. Have them line up on one side of the room and put the buckets of ping pong balls on the other side of the room *(one bucket should be directly across from each team)*.

Step #3: Give each team an empty egg carton.
Say: In this relay-race style game, one person will run to your team's bucket, grab a ping pong ball and bring it back to the team. They will tag the next person in line, who will run and do the same thing. Using the egg carton, you will put the ping pong balls in the correct order so it spells out the memory verse for today. The reference can go at the beginning or the end. You can put the balls in order as you get them or wait until you have gathered them all from the bucket. A few of you might have to run twice.

Step #4: Make sure everyone is lined up and behind the starting line. Let the race begin! The first team to put the verse in order wins.

Wrap-up: Excellent racing everyone! Using your ping pong balls and egg cartons, let's say the verse as a group a few times together! Does anyone think they can say the verse on their own without looking at anything? *(Allow kids to try).* Nice work. Remember, whenever you are afraid, you can trust in God.

Supplies:

- Ping pong balls
- Permanent marker
- Empty egg carton – one for each team
- Large area to run
- Buckets or bowls – one for each team

LEARNING STYLES	TYPE	
KINESTHETIC	GAME	VERSATILE

Bible Stories for Activities 2 and 3
- Romans 15:13 May the God of hope fill you with all joy and peace
- Luke 1 Mary trusted God even when she was afraid
- Psalm 84:12 Blessed is the man who trusts in the Lord
- Proverbs 3:5-6 Trust in the Lord with all your heart

Supplies:

- Reproducible of Psalm 56:3 on page 194.
- Cardstock
- Scissors
- Zippered plastic bags (for kids to take puzzles home in)

LEARNING STYLES	TYPE
LOGICAL	PUZZLE

Optional:

Turn this activity into a fun art project after you are done completing the puzzle. Glue the puzzle pieces onto a piece of construction paper, leaving just a bit of space between each piece for a fun effect.

Activity 3

Puzzle Verse

Step #1: Make a copy of the reproducible page for each child, using cardstock for extra sturdiness.

Say: Our verse today is all about trusting the Lord. Has there ever been a time when you were afraid and trusted in the Lord? What do you do when you are afraid? You can sing when you are afraid or pray – knowing that God will always be with you. We can trust him, even when we can't see that he is with us.

Step #2: Pass out a Psalm 56:3 page to each child and have them cut along the solid black lines, creating a puzzle. Have them mix up the pieces and then complete the puzzle.

Step #3: When everyone has their puzzle assembled, read the verse together as a group. If you have extra time, have kids complete the puzzle again racing against each other.

Wrap-up: This was an interesting way to learn a memory verse! Thankfully, we don't have to be puzzled about God. We know that he is always with us - especially when we are afraid. This week, if you are fearful about something, I encourage you to take your fears to God and ask him to be with you. You can trust him.

At-Home Activity

Hello! Today, we began to learn Psalm 56:3 as a group (see verse below). This week, you can keep learning the verse as a family.

Step #1: Write the verse on a mirror with a dry erase marker or crayon.

Step #2: Each day, erase one word.

Step #3: Encourage family members to say the verse out loud anytime they see it, filling in the missing words as they go.

When I am afraid, I put my trust in you. - Psalm 56:3

Chapter 48

Cast your cares on the LORD and he will sustain you; he will never let the righteous be shaken. – Psalm 55:22

Theme:
God wants to take care of his children.

Overview:
When we pray to God about our concerns, he will give us peace and help us through them.

Supplies:
- Balloons (one for each child, plus extra)
- Clear, open space for kids to walk around in

LEARNING STYLES	TYPE
KINESTHETIC	GAME

Activity 1

Won't Let the Righteous Fall

Step #1: Give each child a balloon and have them blow it up. You may need to help the younger kids.

Say: Today, we're learning a verse from the book of Psalms. Let me read it to you *(Read Psalm 55:22 from your Bible)*. This verse says that God will not let the righteous be shaken. When you are righteous, this means that you love God and you try your best to obey his commands. God will not let the righteous be shaken or fall to destruction. In this game, we're going to make sure that our balloons do not fall to destruction either.

Step #2: Have kids stand up and hold their balloons in their hands. On your mark, kids will toss their balloons up in the air. They must continue hitting their balloon up in the air, making sure it does not touch the ground.

Step #3: Allow kids to keep hitting their balloon until it touches the ground. When it does, they are to pick up their balloon and sit along the wall. The last person to keep their balloon up in the air wins.

Step #4: If you want to increase the difficulty, have kids try to keep 2 balloons up in the air at the same time!

Wrap-up: It isn't always easy to keep those balloons up in the air, is it? Aren't you glad that God is a lot better at keeping us from falling than we are at keeping these balloons from falling? We can trust God and take all our concerns to him. Let's say the verse a few times as a group together.

Bible Stories for This Activity

- Philippians 4:6 Do not be anxious about anything…
- Psalm 37:5 Commit your ways to the Lord. Trust in him, and he will act.

Cast Your Cares (Bean Bag Toss)

Step #1: Prepare the game board. Using the puffy paint, write point values on each of the cups (5, 10, 20 etc). When the paint is dry, glue cups to the board or piece of cardboard, keeping the smaller score in the front and the larger score numbers in the back.

Step #2: Gather the kids together and introduce the verse.
Say: We are learning a verse today about how God takes care of us. Let me read it for you. *(Read Psalm 55:22)*. This verse tells us that we can cast our cares on the Lord.

Step #3: Hold up a bean bag or ping pong ball.
Say: What is a care (or worry) you might have? *(Allow answers)*. Good answers – I have had some of those cares myself. Today, we're going to practice casting our cares. This means that we throw them away from us. We're going to toss bean bags (or ping pong balls) into the cups.

Step #4: Line kids up *(may want to put some kind of mark on the floor for them to stand behind)*. Allow each child to toss 5 bean bags or ping pong balls into the cup. Keep track of score. When kids are done throwing, give them a chance to say the memory verse for bonus points.

Step #5: When everyone has had a chance to throw, tally up the score. Announce a winner.

Wrap-up: You guys really did a good job casting your cares! When we cast our cares on the Lord, he's happy to take them from us – removing worry and fear from our lives. Sometimes we start to worry again, so we have to cast our cares again. The more we trust God with our lives, the easier it will become to cast our cares on him. We know that we can trust God because he wants to take care of us.

Supplies:

- Large plastic cups
- Board or piece of cardboard
- Hot glue gun and glue
- Puffy paint
- Ping pong balls or bean bags

LEARNING STYLES	TYPE
KINESTHETIC	GAME

Bible Stories for Activities 2 and 3

- Psalm 9:10 Those who know your name trust in you…
- 1 Peter 5:7 Cast all your cares on him, because he cares for you.
- Daniel 6:23 No wound was found on [Daniel]
- 1 Samuel 1:10-18 Hannah casts her cares on the Lord

Supplies:

- Large area for kids to run around in
- Poster of Psalm 55:22

LEARNING STYLES   TYPE

KINESTHETIC   GAME   VERSATILE

Send a copy of the "verse treasure hunt" paper on page 198 home with families

Duck, Duck, Verse!

Step #1: Have kids sit in a circle on the floor.

Say: Our verse today is all about trusting the Lord with our cares and worries. Let's read it together. *(You or a child read Psalm 55:22).* Have you ever been worried about something? Let's spend a few minutes now, praying and casting our cares on the Lord, just as our verse tells us.

Step #2: Show kids the poster of Psalm 55:22. Select a volunteer to be the first "it" in the game.

Say: n this game, we are going to play something like "Duck, Duck, Goose". However, instead of saying "Duck, Duck…" you will say the words of the verse – one word for each child. You will start with the reference and end with the word "shaken". Whoever's head you touch when you say the word "shaken" will get up and chase you around the circle – just like Duck, Duck, Goose.

Step #3: Play a few rounds of the game, making the poster easily seen in case kids need it for reference.

Wrap-up: This was an interesting way to learn a memory verse! Does anyone want to try to say the verse on their own (allow kids to try). Nice work! I'm so glad that I can cast my cares on God, knowing that he will care for me.

At-Home Activity

Hello! Today, we began to learn Psalm 55:22 as a group (see verse below). This verse tells us that we can give our worries over to God and he will take care of us. This week, review as a family by playing a game of "Verse Treasure Hunt".

Step #1: Cut apart the words from the "Verse Treasure Hunt" page.
Step #2: Hide the words throughout the house.
Step #3: Have the kids search throughout the house to find all the words.
Step #4: Assemble the verse as a family. If there are words missing, send the kids to find the rest until the verse is complete.
Step #5 Once the verse is reassembled, say the verse together as a family.

Cast your cares on the LORD and he will sustain you; he will never let the righteous be shaken.
- Psalm 55:22

Chapter 48 - Verse Treasure Hunt

Cast your cares on

the LORD and he

will sustain you; he

will never let the

righteous be

shaken. Psalm 55:22

Chapter 49

By this everyone will know that you are my disciples, if you love one another.
- John 13:35

Overview:
When we show God's love to others, they see God in us.

Supplies:

- Pony beads
- Alphabet beads
- Plastic lacing cord, yarn, or pipe cleaners

LEARNING STYLES	TYPE
TACTILE	CRAFT

Activity 1

Love One Another (Bead Bracelets)

Step #1: Introduction
Say: Today, we're going to be learning a verse from the book of John. John is one of the four Gospels. The Gospels tell us about Jesus's time on earth. The book of John contains a lot of the teachings of Jesus, including some instructions that he gave to his disciples, his closest friends. Jesus said that we will show people that we love Jesus when we love each other. It's not always easy to love one another, so today, we're going to make a bracelet that will remind us of this verse.

Step #2: Place the beads within easy reach of the kids and pass out yarn or cords for making bracelets. Pipe cleaners work great for little hands.

Step #3: Encourage kids to use the alphabet beads to spell "Love One Another" on their bracelets.

Wrap-up: Great job on these bracelets guys! Let's practice the verse together a few times as we finish up with our bracelets.

Bible Stories for This Activity

- John 15:12 Love each other as I have loved you.
- 1 John 3:11 Love one another

Activity 2

Stick Some Love On You!

Supplies:

- Painters tape or cellopane tape
- Heart hole puncher or small heart template from chapter 9
- Colored card stock
- Large playing area for running
- Timer

Step #1: Before the group arrives, cut out hearts (at least 3 per child) and place a tape loop on each one.

Step #2: Set hearts on table (tape side up) in the playing area. **Say:** Today, we're learning a verse from the Gospel of John. This book was written by John, who was one of Jesus's disciples. John tells us about the things Jesus did and the things Jesus said. One of the things that Jesus told his followers to do was to love one another. That's our verse for today. Let's read it together *(Read John 13:35 from your Bible)*. Let's say that together *(Lead kids in saying the verse)*. We're going to play a little game where we're going to give each other some love.

Step #3: Show kids one of the hearts and explain the game. **Say:** The object of this game is to give away as much love as you can. When the game begins, you will head to the heart table and grab one (and only one) heart. You must try to stick it on the back of another player. After you have a heart on your back, you can try to get it off to pass it on to another player, but it might not be easy. After you have given away your first heart, you can head to the table for another. In order to win, you want to give away all the love (hearts), but not get any on your own back. At the end of one minute, whoever has the LEAST amount of hearts on their back wins.

Step #4: Set the timer for one minute and allow kids to play the game. At the end of the round, count up the hearts and declare a winner. Say the verse as a group as you place the hearts back on the table. Play again as time permits.

Wrap-up: That was a lot of love traveling around out there on the playing field! Showing love to others, of course, isn't as easy as sticking a paper heart on someone's back. How are ways we can show love to one another in real life? *(Allow kids to answer)*. Great answers! Let's practice John 13:35 one more time!

LEARNING STYLES	TYPE

KINESTHETIC	GAME

Bible Stories for Activities 2 and 3

- Mark 12:31 Love your neighbor
- Luke 6:35 Love your enemies, do good to them
- 1 John 4:20-21 You cannot love God and hate your brother
- 1 John 2:10 Whoever loves his brother abides in the light

Supplies:

- Premade sugar cookies, in the shape of a heart
- Frosting, various colors
- Plastic knives
- Sprinkles or other cookie decoration
- Pre-decorated cookie
- Love Verse Match Up sheet on page 202 (optional)

LEARNING STYLES	TYPE
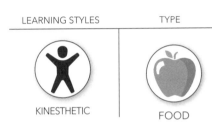 KINESTHETIC	FOOD

Activity 3

Cookie Craft

Step #1: Show kids your pre-decorated cookie.

Say: We're going to learn about a verse today in a very tasty way. Can anyone guess what our verse might be about? *(Allow answers)*. If you guessed love, you are correct! Today's verse comes from the book of John. Would anyone like to read John 13:35 for me? *(Allow someone to read the verse from their Bible)*. Jesus gave his disciples a lot of instructions while he was on earth, and this was one of them. He said it was very important to love one another. Can you think of some ways that we can love one another? *(Allow answers)*.

Step #2: Pass out cookies (one per child) and make the frosting and decorations easily available. Encourage kids to decorate their cookies and let them know they will be giving them away at the end in order to show love.

Step #3: Once everyone is done decorating, have kids give cookies to each other (making sure everyone gets one in the end).

Step #4: If you have extra time, have kids complete the love verse match up sheet.

Wrap-up: Nice work today on that decorating! One way we can show love to others is serving them or baking them a tasty treat. This week, I would encourage you to look for more ways that you can show love to the people in your life.

At-Home Activity

Hello! Today, we talked about John 13:35 with the group. If we have chosen to follow Jesus with our lives, we are a disciple of Christ. This verse tells us that other people will know that we are a disciple of Christ when we love one another. Sometimes, the hardest people to love are the people closest to us! This week, you are encouraged to show extra love to those in your family. Some ideas include:

- Giving someone a hug when they come home
- Giving someone a compliment on something they did well
- Drawing a picture or writing a note and hiding it in a lunchbox or briefcase
- Pick or buy flowers for someone (or balloons for the kids!)
- Tell someone, "I really like you!"

The best place to practicing loving one another is in your own home. Enjoy some love this week!

By this everyone will know that you are my disciples, if you love one another. - John 13:35

Chapter 49 - Love Verse Match Up

Draw a line from the verse reference to the matching verse

♥	Romans 12:9
♥	John 3:16
♥	Mark 12:31
♥	Romans 13:10
♥	1 Peter 4:8
♥	1 John 4:7
♥	Matthew 22:37
♥	John 15:9
♥	Psalm 63:3
♥	1 John 4:19:
♥	Exodus 34:6
♥	Joshua 23:1
♥	Psalm 36:7

♥	*Love your neighbor as yourself*
♥	*Love must be sincere*
♥	*Love each other deeply*
♥	*Remain in my love.*
♥	*For God so loved the world…*
♥	*Love is from God.*
♥	*Love does no harm to a neighbor*
♥	*Love God with all your heart…*
♥	*We love because he [God] first loved us*
♥	*How priceless is your unfailing love, O God!*
♥	*So be very careful to love the Lord your God.*
♥	*Your steadfast love is better than life.*
♥	*The Lord is abounding in love.*

Chapter 50

But God demonstrates his own love for us in this: While we were still sinners, Christ died for us. - Romans 5:8

Theme:
God gave us salvation through Jesus's death.

Overview:
God loves us so much he sacrificed his own son for us.

Supplies:

- Pieces of construction paper
- Heart template from page 14 (ch 2)
- Wall for hanging hearts
- Markers or crayons

LEARNING STYLES	TYPE
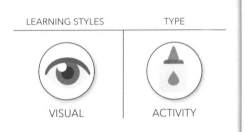	
VISUAL	ACTIVITY

Activity 1

God Shows Us Love (Heart Display)

Step #1: Introduction.

Say: Today, we're going to be learning a verse from the book of Romans. This is a great verse for us to learn and memorize because it shows how much God really loves us. Let me read it to you *(Read Romans 5:8 from your Bible to the kids)*. Isn't it amazing that while we were still sinners *(and not wanting a relationship with God),* that Christ died for us? Wow. That's some pretty powerful love. Today, we're going to make a display to remind us about how much God loves us.

Step #2: Pass out construction paper and heart templates to the kids. Instruct them to cut a heart from their construction paper and then write the verse inside of it. If they finish early, they can make extra hearts that say things like "God loves you" or "God shows us love".

Step #3: Help kids to hang hearts on the wall.

Wrap-up: God is amazing! I'm so glad that he chose to love us and save us from our sins, even when we didn't deserve it. Let's spend some time praying and thanking God for sending his son, Jesus, to pay for our sins.

Bible Stories for This Activity

- John 15:13 Greater love has no man… lay down his life
- John 3:16 God so loved the world, that he gave his one and only son…

Tape Resist Water Color Cross

Step #1: Set up supplies at each chair before kids arrive. Each place should have one piece of paper, a watercolor palette, a brush, small cup of water, and smock (optional).

Say: Hello, everyone! Today, we're going to take a closer look at a verse from the book of Romans. This book was written by the apostle Paul and it was written to the believers in Rome. In this chapter, we learn about the good news of salvation. Even before we had done anything to deserve it, God sent his son, Jesus, to die for our sins. Romans 5:8 tells us that while we were still sinners, Christ died for us. That's a pretty big deal. God gave us a gift we didn't deserve at all – forgiveness and the promise of living with God forever in heaven. Today, we're going to make a craft that reminds us of Jesus's death on the cross so that we can have this gift from God.

Step #2: Demonstrate how to make a cross shape in the middle of the paper with the painter's tape. Instruct kids to paint the rest of the paper with their water colors. Painting in wide, diagonal stripes creates a wonderful effect.

Step #3: After kids are finished painting, remove the painter's tape to reveal a white cross shape.

Step #4: Once the watercolor has dried, instruct kids to write "Romans 5:8" inside the cross.

Wrap-up: These are beautiful works of art, reminding us of the beautiful gift that God has given us! Let's practice this verse together a few times.

Supplies:

- Painters tape
- Watercolors and paint brushes
- Water
- Smocks (optional)
- Heavy paper (watercolor paper, ideally)
- Fine tip permanent marker
- Sample craft (optional)

LEARNING STYLES	TYPE
TACTILE	ACTIVITY

Bible Stories for Activities 2 and 3

- 1 Peter 3:18 Jesus suffered for our sins, to bring us closer to God
- Romans 4:25 Jesus was delivered to death for our sins
- 2 Corinthians 6:2 Today is the day of salvation
- Ephesians 2:4-5 God is rich in mercy….made us alive in Christ

Supplies:

- Copy of Romans 5:8 page 206 (one for each child)
- Crayons
- Construction paper
- Glue
- Laminator and laminating pouches (optional)
- Zip-type bags (optional)

LEARNING STYLES	TYPE
LOGICAL	PUZZLE

Activity 3

God's Love Puzzle

Step #1: Pass out the Romans 5:8 page to the kids along with some crayons. Instruct kids to color in the hearts as you talk about the verse.

Say: Our verse today comes from the book Romans and it has some very good news. Would anyone like to read the verse from your page? *(Allow a volunteer to read).* Wow. God did not wait until we were totally good, or until we stopped making mistakes in our life. This verse tells us that while we were still sinners, Christ died for us. That's some big love! Today, we're going to make a puzzle to remind us of our verse and hopefully help us learn it too!

Step #2: After kids have finished coloring the Romans 5:8 page, have them glue it to a piece of construction paper. If desired, run the page through the laminator for extra durability.

Step #3: Instruct kids to cut page into smaller pieces, to create their own type of puzzle.

Step #4: Mix up the pieces and see if they can piece their page back together. After they are finished assembling the puzzle, have them store it inside a zip-type bag.

Wrap-up: Nice work today on the puzzles! I'm so glad that God's love isn't a puzzle to us. The Bible tells us that God gives salvation freely to anyone who asks. I wonder if you have made a decision to follow Jesus in your life? If not, today is a great day to turn from your sins and receive God's free gift of salvation!

** Would work with any verse **

At-Home Activity

Hello! Today in class, we talked about Romans 5:8 (read it below). This verse gives such a clear picture of God's love for us. God's love is based on his own mercy and grace, and nothing that we have done. This week, you are encouraged to continue learning this verse as a family.

Step #1: Write each word of the verse on a separate sticky note.
Step #2: Place the notes along a hall or going up the stairs.
Step #3: As you pass by the words, make it a point to say them out loud.
Step #4: Each day, take down one word of the verse (start at the beginning of the verse) and see if each member of the family can still complete the verse correctly.
Step #5: When all the words are gone, celebrate learning a new verse as a family!

But God demonstrates his own love for us in this: While we were still sinners, Christ died for us.
– Romans 5:8

"BUT GOD DEMONSTRATES HIS OWN LOVE FOR US IN THIS: WHILE WE WERE STILL SINNERS, CHRIST DIED FOR US."

ROMANS 5:8

Index

THEME:

TYPE:
Games:

Crafts:

Activity:

Music:

Object Lesson:
For more Object Lessons see our book: Top 50 Object Lessons

Puzzle:

Food:

Versatile:
CAN BE USED WITH ANY VERSE!

LEARNING STYLE
Verbal:

Auditory:

Kinesthetic:

Visual:

Tactile:

Logical:

Top 50 Object Lessons

208 pages, 8-⅜" x 11" Paperback, Black & White Illustrations

The RoseKidz **Top 50 series** continues with the next book in the series, **Top 50 Object Lessons** are vital to hide God's Word in the heart and mind of every child. This book is packed with fun, interactive, creative and engaging ways to get children excited about memorizing Scripture. The 50 verses are in an easy-to-learn format.

| Top 50 Object Lessons | R50009 | 978-1-628625-04-2 |

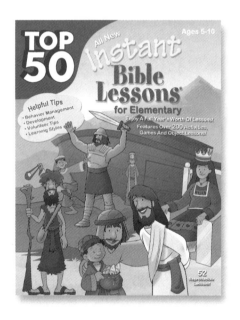

Top 50 Instant Bible Lessons

Ages 5–10, 256 pages, 8-⅜" x 11" Paperback, Black & White Illustrations

The **Top 50 Series** is a NEW reproducible resource for churches that want children to know and remember the **Top 50 Bible stories**. Includes a whole year's worth of lessons, combining some fresh new lessons with hand-selected lessons from favorite RoseKidz products (previously Rainbow Press). Enjoy the quick and easy-to-use reproducible resources packed with lessons, activities and crafts. Includes top lessons every child should know. Volunteer and child-friendly!

| Top 50 Instant Bible Lessons for Elementary | R50003 | 9781628624984 |

24 Easy-To-Do

256 pages, 8-⅜" x 11" Paperback, Black & White Illustrations

This new **24 Easy-To-Do Family Ministry Holiday Events** book helps create events at church for families to come together once a month! You and your family will learn to apply God's Word to your weekly lives, while creating connections & Christian traditions for each holiday season! Each event offers insight for the Children and Family Ministry team to encourage and support, while giving practical hands-on experiences and resources for families to carry on past the event. Includes take home materials to offer families an easy to use way of doing family devotions on their own, while reinforcing the learning. This is a great resource to help children's ministry leaders create opportunities for families to embrace their God given mission to be the spiritual teachers of their children.

| 24 Easy-To-Do Family Ministry Holiday Events | R50012 | 9781628625189 |

Find more great stuff by visiting our website: **www. HendricksonRose.com**